Treasures Underfoot

Quilting with Manhole Covers

Round 2

The Carriage Trade Press

P.O. Box 51491-Eugene, OR 97405

http://www.carriagetradepress.com

Threasures Underfoot
Quilting With Manhole Covers
Round 2

Cover Design: Shirley MacGregor
                            Joe Ferrare
Color Graphics: Joe Ferrare
Photography: Shirley MacGregor
Calligraphy: Masaru Aniya

The
Carriage Trade
Press

Copyright© 2001 by Shirley MacGregor
Published by The Carriage Trade Press
PO Box 51491, Eugene, Oregon 97405
http://www.carriagetradepress.com
email: info@carriagetradepress.com

ISBN 0-9671433-6-5

Printend in the Republic of Korea
by
Ulchi Gracom Ltd.
email: gunngook@hitel.net

Dedication
The book is dedicated to the memory of my mother, Vivian Spowers Hoffman, and to Larry Crehan.

Acknowledgements
To all the quilt artist who have so generously shared there time, energy, and dedicated their quilts to make this book possible.

Special Thanks
Sheila Steers for her tireless effort and support on so many levels, and especially for being a true friend.

Douglas MacGregor, my husband, for all his help and dedication to making this book become a reality.

Pat Hann, and *Sachiko Nagaishi* for coordinating project assignments in the UK and Japan.

Masaru Aniya, and the Embassy of Japan, Seoul, for initial display of the quilts in this book.

Editing
Douglas MacGregor, Sheila Steers, Judy Bartran, Connie Antonelli and Joe Ferrare.

Graphics
Joe Ferrare, whose incredible graphic effects make the pages come alive.

Masaru Aniya for his beautiful calligraphy.

Translation and Communication
Yong Sik Kim, Dong Won Yu, Masaru Aniya and Ok Sun Chang.

Sound Advice and Moral Support
Barbara Eikmeier and *Kim Hey-Suk*

And to anyone I have left out, my most profound apology.

Outline/Index

Acknowledgements

Table of contents

I.   Preface

II.   Introduction

III.   Japan Notes

IV.   Manhole Covers

V. Footnotes

A good deal of water has passed under the streets of Japan since the idea for "Quilting With Manhole Covers" came to me. And what an adventure it has been! For those of you who are not familiar with my first publishing effort, I will try to give you an idea of how it came about.

When my husband was assigned to The Sullivans School at Yokosuka Naval Base, Japan, in the fall of 1994, we settled in the pleasant seaside community of Zushi. While out for early morning jogs I often admired the beautiful design work on the city's manhole covers. I thought it would make a great design for a quilt, and filed it away in my mind for future reference.

As time went by and I moved about the area, I noticed other interesting designs on manhole covers in neighboring communities. Two in particular caught my eye, and one day I set out with friend to brave the crowded streets to secure rubbings for a pattern.

I made a quilt entirely in silk, and called it "Treasures Underfoot." When it managed a 1st place at the Pacific International Quilt Expo, I was truly inspired.

Meanwhile, the number of manhole cover sightings increased, along with my admiration for these beautifully fashioned, 100-pound disks. The designs were just too good to leave lying in the streets. That's when the idea of a book occurred to me.

In the ensuing months, I enlisted the aid of some of my Japanese friends and began gathering data for a possible publication. My investigations took me to city offices, iron foundries, and to an ever-widening circle of cities and towns, in search of interesting manhole covers.

It seems appropriate to note here that my sanity was definitely in question during this period of discovery, especially by the natives. Most had never even noticed the designs on their manhole covers, and to many, looking to the streets for artistic inspiration just wasn't an option. But the Japanese are very gracious and accommodating, and my friends stuck with me through thick and thin.

To test the waters, I sent a few of the manhole cover designs to friends in the US to use as quilt themes. They willingly complied, and asked for more! The book idea was raised to the next level.

My husband and I printed some sample pages and sent a proposal to several publishing houses, both in Japan and the United States. From the outset, the responses we received were encouraging. The publishers found the theme quite unique, and indicated that there was indeed a potential market for the designs. However, all felt that such a book would not produce sufficient profit to warrant their involvement. Two suggested that we self-publish.

We had arrived at a difficult juncture: either use our limited resources to produce a book that just might pay for itself, or swallow hard and let the idea die gracefully. We agonized over this dilemma for a good ten minutes, and decided to go for it.

By this time, we had moved across the East Sea to Seoul, South Korea, which added a whole new dimension to the project. Although I had gathered most of the essential material for the book, I would now have to rely on friends to pick up the loose ends that were bound to appear. But with my dedicated helpers, and with the indispensable Internet and e-mail, the pieces fell into place in reasonable fashion.

In Seoul I located an eager young design team to handle the graphics, and a knowledgeable printer whose wise counsel kept the project on course. *Quilting With Manhole Covers* was published at the end of May, 1999, and shortly thereafter 3,000 copies, neatly boxed, arrived at our apartment. Thus began a new, more cramped, phase of the adventure.

The book has done well, thanks to effort and support of a great many people, a lot of hard work, and more than a little luck. It was indeed a very satisfying experience, and continues to provide an enormous amount of satisfaction.

Two years on, I couldn't help but hear the mournful sounds of all those yet-to-be-discovered manhole covers, lying helplessly in the streets of Japan, and set to work once again. Here are more Treasures Underfoot – please take them in and give them a new life in cloth.

I hope that *Treasures Underfoot* inspires you, for that is its purpose. Although it is clearly not a how-to book, I feel obliged to offer a comment or two (you might call them biases) on translating these manhole cover designs into quilts. For those new to quilting, I have also included a few suggestions that should be helpful in a variety of quilting projects.

A unique feature of this book is that it allows you to look at a given design in three very different renditions – silhouette, stylized design, and finished quilt. And if you read the comments made by the quilt artists, you may find yet another dimension to ponder. I would encourage you to explore these features as you develop a project concept.

Quilt artists whose work appears in the book received just the black and white silhouette of the design to work from. There were no directions, stipulations, suggestions or even hints at what I expected of them. They were totally free to choose, and so are you.

At the foundries, where these interesting designs are cast in iron, the artists are constrained by the physical requirements of the manhole cover. Function, durability, and a preordained shape provide a very challenging medium for the designers. But you are free to take these concepts in any direction you wish.

Alternative Shapes

Most manhole covers are round out of practicality. A round disk, slightly larger than the hole it covers, will not fall through; other shapes will. You probably won't have that problem, so you can pull your design into any shape that strikes your fancy. Squash it, bloat it, take the rim off, and it will still be there! The Matusyama design (page 43) and the Yokkaichi design (page 124) are good examples. Making an oval or elongating the design can add an interesting dimension to your project. Pat Hann's interpretation of the Mine City design (page 46) is a radical departure from the basic shape, but still maintains the spiral configuration of the original.

Dissolving Borders

Just because the design is confined within a circular border doesn't mean that you have to leave it there. Sheila Steers in her "River Warrior's Game" (page 114) has cleverly distorted the rim while maintaining the circular design within. If you look at the two interpretations of the Nagasaki design, you'll notice the that hydrangeas have been freed from their circular confinement.

Playing with the Theme

Many of the manhole cover designs have multiple themes, and of course you are free to choose any aspect or feature as the focus of your quilt project. Or you can follow the lead of Sheila Steers and Paul Wank and change the game entirely. Sheila obviously had something else in mind as she crafted the Naha design (page 69). And in the Otaru design (page 102) Paul's cats have clearly upstaged the otters.

You might scale down a design and use it as a feature in a larger theme, or perhaps bring a minor feature to the forefront. Mi Oak Kwon took what could have been a rather ho-hum design (Niigata, page 88) and dropped a fantastic vegetable garden right in the middle. The possibilities are only limited by your imagination.

Color Choices

The operative phrase once again is *Don't Limit Yourself*. The foundry artists are at something of a disadvantage in this respect, as iron usually comes in a few shades of gray, and of course rust. And painting each cover is certainly not a common practice as the cars would wear the paint off in no time. Lucky for you, traffic over your cover will be considerably less, so you can apply color freely! Remember, things are often more dramatic, and definitely more noticeable when portrayed in colors that are more or less than what nature intended.

Notes for "Newbies"

If you are new to quilting I have a few suggestions to offer. I would call them rules, but that sounds a bit "preachy."

Recently I heard an accomplished guitarist give this advice: "If you want to play better, play with a group of other musicians." I couldn't think of any better advice to offer a new quilter. Join a quilt group or get together with other quilters on a regular basis. You will be surprised at how such interaction will help you to grow.

Color

Here is something I always stress when working with new students: use a combination of light, medium and dark colors, and arrange them so that the values shift noticeably. You can test your color combinations by standing back and squinting, or better yet, by laying a red plastic sheet over your grouping. Both methods will diminish the impact of the colors and allow you to concentrate on value.

Fabrics

Choosing fabrics is as important as combining colors, and really the two go hand in hand. Learn to use small, medium and large (really large) prints in combination. Such combinations can make the difference between a "nice" quilt and "fantastic" one. Use stripes, plaids, anything and everything. There's no such thing as a bad fabric (well, almost).

Executing Your Design

There was a time when a "real quilter" stuck to traditional designs and only quilted by hand. Times have changed and modern quilting takes many forms. Try your hand at as many of these methods as possible, and use as wide a variety of materials as you can. Remember, the goal is enjoyment and satisfaction.

Japan is a chain of mountainous islands lying off the East-Asian coast. Its closest neighbors are China, Korea and Russia. In size, it is a bit larger than Italy, with a population approaching 125 million.

The country is divided into nine administrative regions. Hokkaido, the large, northernmost island, is one of these. Moving south to the main island of Honshu are the Tohoku, Chubo, Kanto, Kinki and Chugoku regions. Further to the southeast are the island regions of Shikoku and Kyushu, and finally Okinawa region, which is a string of smaller islands well to the southeast.

Within the regions are 47 prefectures, which are roughly equivalent to US counties, or in some cases, states. An example of the administrative structure would be Yokohama, which is located on the main island of Honshu, in the Kanto region, in Kanagawa Prefecture.

The history of Japan is broken down into 13 periods, 10 of which are listed below to give the reader some perspective on dates mentioned in the text. Dates vary depending on the source.

Nara – mid-500's - 794	Edo -Tokugawa – 1600 - 1867
Heian – 794 - 1185	Meiji – 1868 – 1912
Kamakura – 1185 - 1335	Taisho – 1912 - 1926
Muromachi – 1335 – mid-1570's	Showa – 1926 -1989
Azuchi – Momoyama – mid-1570's – 1600	Heisei – 1989 – present

TheKamakura Period

Probably the most colorful era of Japanese history, and the one that is most familiar to westerners, is the feudal Kamakura period. This was the time of the shugun – or military leader – whose will was enforced by the privileged samurai warriors. It is also the time that Zen Buddhism took root in Japan.

The Edo Period

During the Edo period, Japan was ruled by the Tokugawa clan. It was a time of peace, seclusion from the outside world, and little change. Much of what those in western countries view as traditional Japanese art and culture comes from this time. Toward the end of the Edo period, US Commodore Matthew Perry arrived on the scene and demanded that Japan open its ports to trade with the West.

The Tokaido

Throughout the book you will see references to the Tokaido. Tokaido means "Eastern Sea Road," and in feudal times it was the main route between Edo (Tokyo) and Kyoto, which was the capitol prior to 1600. On a map of Japan, trace along the coast from Tokyo, through Yokohama and Kamakura, to Shizuoka, on to Nagoya and finally up to Kyoto. The road was a very narrow, tree-lined track, strictly controlled, and for security reasons, limited to foot traffic. Those journeying along the Tokaido were required to have passports as they traveled between jurisdictions. Many important temples and shrines, as well as other significant relics of the time, may still be found along this route.

If you are interested in learning more about Japan, there are a great many books available about the county and its people. For a casual look, travel books have well-written "nutshell" commentaries on Japan's history and culture. There are also many excellent Internet sites - some sponsored by government tourist offices, others by amateurs - that cover a wide variety of topics.

Better still, you should make a point to visit Japan. Put aside any biases or fears you might have and go; you won't be disappointed. It is truly a fascinating country, safe and clean, and its people are among the most accommodating you will find anywhere in the world. Expensive? Yes, but you can work around that with a little effort.

Japan Notes

Below I have included a small map to help you zero in on the communities represented in the book. I would suggest using a larger map to better understand the geographical features of each location. If you plan your travels on my map, you are in for a big surprise!

Cities Represented

1 - Aizu Wakamatsu
2 - Fuji City
3 - Hadano City
4 - Himeji City
5 - Hirokami Village
6 - Iwankuni City
7 - Matsudo City
8 - Matsumoto City
9 - Matsuyama City
10 - Mine City
11 - Nagayo Town
12 - Nagaokakyo City
13 - Nagasaki City
14 - Nagoya City

15 - Naha City
16 - Nakatsu City
17 - Nara City
18 - Narashino City
19 - Niigata City
20 - Otaru City
21 - Otsu City
22 - Takamatsu City
23 - Tsuruoka City
24 - Yokkaichi City
25 - Yamaguchi City
26 - Yao City
27 - Yokosuka City

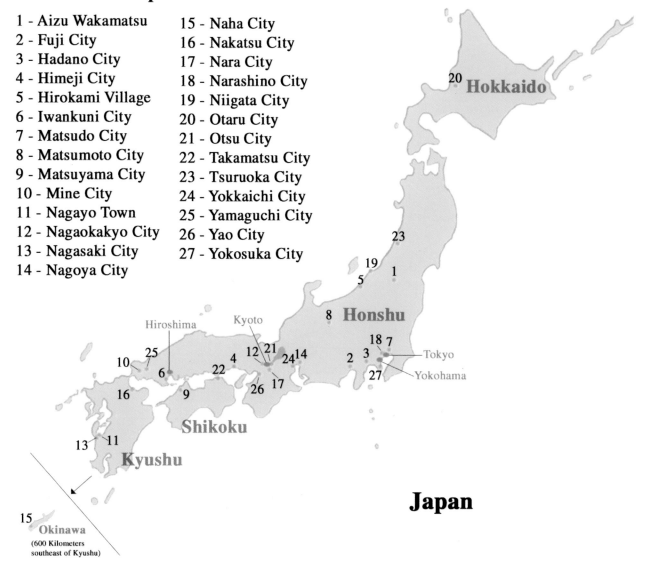

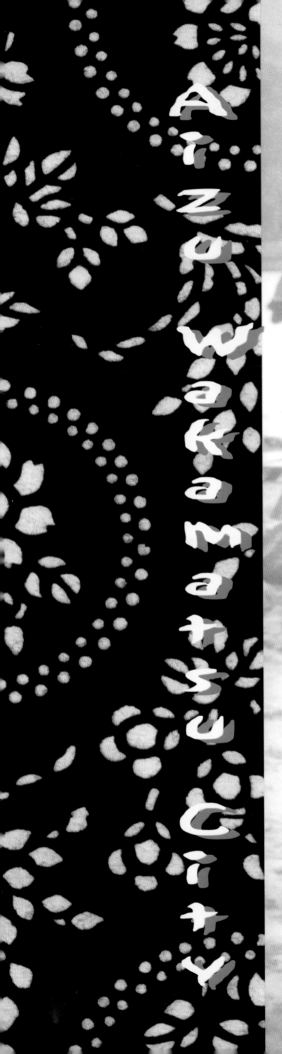

Aizu Wakamatsu is, first and foremost, a castle town, with its identity tied tightly to the events and images of its romantic past. It celebrated 100 years as an incorporated city in 1999, but its history reaches back to ancient times. The original castle dates back to 1390, when it was a stronghold for the Aizu clan.

In 1590, by order of Shogun Hideoshi Toyotomi, the existing castle was replaced with a more ambitious structure, complete with a 7-story tower. This impressive tower was said to resemble a crane (long a symbol of purity and longevity in Japanese tradition), thus the castle was named Tsuguro-jo, or crane castle. Today, when the cherry trees are in full blossom, you would do well to find a more beautiful sight than the grounds of Tsuguro-jo.

For history buffs, Aizu Wakamatsu offers one of the most compelling stories of feudal Japan to be found. Fascinating tales of courage, loyalty and sacrifice in the highest Japanese tradition abound. It was here that the Byakko-tai (White Tiger Brigade, composed of 16 and 17 year old boys) and the Joshi-gun (a brigade of young women trained in the martial arts) made their heroic last stand against Imperial forces.

Aizu Wakamatsu is located in the Bandai region of Honshu, about 15 kilometers southwest of Mt. Bandai. The mountain, still considered an active volcano, last erupted in 1888, forming beautiful lakes and spectacular terrain. Today, the area is one of Japan's most popular tourist attractions. Aizu Wakamatsu's manhole cover features Mt. Bandai, and the red pine, which is the city's flower.

Kathy Sperry
"Window on my World"
24" x 24"

"The first glimpse of this design brought back childhood memories, and a smile to my face. I knew immediately what I would do. I grew up in the Willamette Valley (Oregon), where strawberry fields flourished and mountains could be seen in the distance.

For this quilt, I used hand-dyed fabrics, batiks and many other cottons. The background is hand pieced to simulate the sky, earth and grass, with the manhole cover design applied over this using machine appliqué and reverse appliqué. I used metallic and variegated rayon threads in the machine quilting."

Cathy, a secondary school teacher on "extended family leave," lives in Anaheim Hills, California. "I began sewing when I was 11 years old and went on to major in home economics at Oregon State University. I actually started quilting in 1985 in New Jersey 'just to meet people' in a new location. I have never stopped. We relocated six times in 12 years and quilting has been my in-road to instant and lasting friendships." (See footnote 1)

Fuji City

富士市

Fuji City sits at the base of Mt. Fuji, Japan's tallest and most revered mountain. Located on the south side of the mountain, it looks out toward Suruga Bay and the Pacific Ocean. The city is the result of a 1966 incorporation of two smaller communities, but its historical past is colorful, indeed.

In olden times, the city was frequented by samurai who traveled the historic Tokaido Road between Tokyo (then Edo) and Kyoto.

Today, Fuji City has a population of around 235,000 people. Among its varied industries, Fuji City produces a large percentage of Japan's most popular beverage tea. Terraced fields of tea plants, stretch across the base of the mountain, adding to the area's formidable beauty. During harvest time, women in traditional dress may be seen clipping leaves from the plants.

Quite are understandably, the dominant feature. The Fuji City manhole cover is the mountain, with Suruga Bay in the foreground.

Karen Harmony
"Fuji Fantasy"
19.5" dia.

"I work mostly in cotton fabrics, and hand dyed the sky fabric for this quilt. …I almost always find my inspiration in the fabric. My quilt is heavily embellished with beads and crystals from old necklaces."

Karen lives in northwest Arkansas, having moved there recently from the Willamette Valley in Oregon. She began quilting in 1976 during the Bicentennial, and turned professional in 1990. "I have done needlework since I was 17, starting with crewel embroidery, then knitting, needlepoint, and finally added quilting." She "ventured into the world of art quilts in 1996."

[Karen was responsible for bringing the entire collection of manhole cover quilts to Arkansas in 1999 for an exhibition. – Shirley] (See footnote 1.)

Hadano City

秦野市

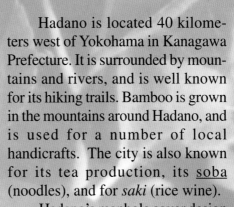

Hadano is located 40 kilometers west of Yokohama in Kanagawa Prefecture. It is surrounded by mountains and rivers, and is well known for its hiking trails. Bamboo is grown in the mountains around Hadano, and is used for a number of local handicrafts. The city is also known for its tea production, its soba (noodles), and for *saki* (rice wine).

Hadano's manhole cover design features the city's symbol in the center, and groups of snails circle the outer rim. Snails were chosen to bring to mind clean water and the friendliness of nature.

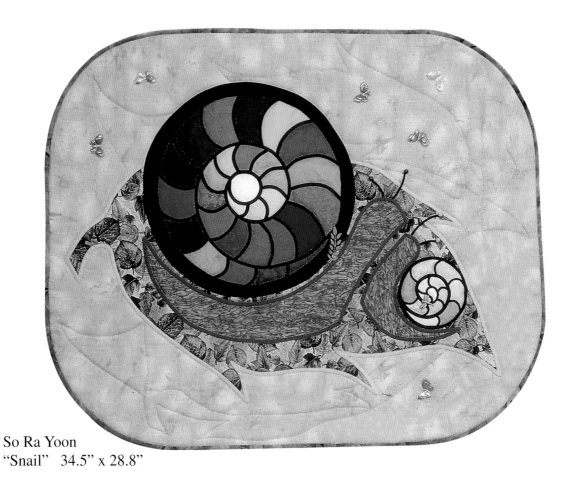

So Ra Yoon
"Snail"   34.5" x 28.8"

For her interpretation of the Hadano City manhole cover design, So Ra used American and Korean fabrics. She lifted one of the snail groupings from the design to feature in her quilt. She embellished it with a number of small iridescent butterflies, and hand quilted, using some metallic threads.

So Ra is a graduate of Kongwon University with a major in Fashion Design. She spent 3 years living in China, where her first child was born, but now lives with her family in Seoul. She has been quilting for five years, and has taken quilting classes in Korea and the United States.

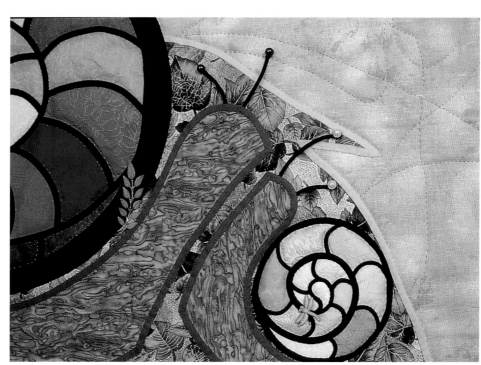

姫路市

Himeji, with a population approaching a half million, is situated on Japan's Inland Sea, in Hyogo Prefecture just west of Kobe. Himeji Castle is the city's virtual heart and soul, and provides it an enviable place in Japanese history.

Himeji-jo is the most complete and most representative of the Japanese castles. It was designated a national treasure in 1931, and achieved recognition as a UNESCO World Culture and Heritage Site in 1993. The initial fortifications on the castle grounds were erected in the late 1500's, but the current structure was begun in 1601. It took nine years, 360 tons of wood, and an enormous effort to complete. The castle was built with formidable defenses, and has a number of clever features designed to deceive an attacking enemy. From the outside, it appears to have just five stories, but actually has six, plus a basement.

Resting serenely on nearby Mt. Shosha is the Engyoji temple complex, which has drawn pilgrims from all over Japan since its founding in the 10th century.

Himeji's manhole cover design features *sagi kusa* grass, the city's flower.

Faye Quayle
"Tribute to Himeji"
66" x 66"

[I measured] "…the manhole cover near our property, and found it about 28" across. I decided my manhole cover would also be about that size... The fabrics I used in my quilt are all cotton, some hand dyed, some marbled. I sashiko quilted the Himeji City design in charcoal-gray thread on a pastel background. This was hand appliquéd on a colorful 'paved street,' composed of a tessellation comprising four pieces in a 2 1/2 inch square. Each little piece had to be 'auditioned' on my pin-up wall - a slow but satisfying process – and then approved by my quilting friends!"

Fay lives in Wellington, New Zealand, with her husband of 50 years. She has been a quilter since 1951, and has "tutored around New Zealand." Her quilts have been exhibited and featured in books and magazines in the United States and Japan, as well as in New Zealand.

Himeji Citiy

HIROKAMI village

広神村

Hirokami stretches out across a river valley forming a beautiful green patchwork of farmland. It is situated in Niigata Prefecture, where a large percentage of Japan's rice is grown.

The Hirokami manhole cover design features the *magubasho*, a lily that appears in the spring when the snow is melting. This flower was chosen because it will grow well only in the purest of water, and thus reflects Hirokami's desire for a clean environment. A ring of small hexagons encircling the flower in the design symbolizes snow flakes, as more snow falls in this region than in any other part of Japan.

Iwakuni City

岩国市

Iwakuni City

Iwakuni City is a historic community located in the eastern part of Yamaguchi Prefecture, a few kilometers southeast of Hiroshima. An important castle town in early times, it is now a modern city of 110,000, and boasts some unique and interesting attractions.

The center point of Iwakuni is the Kentai-kyo bridge, a picturesque five-arch wooden structure that spans the Nishiki river. First built in 1673, the bridge was destroyed by a typhoon in 1950. It was faithfully restored (no nails allowed!) to its original condition three years later.

In summer, cormorant fishermen, dressed in period costume, ply their trade on the calm waters of the Nishiki. This activity is depicted on the city's manhole cover, along with the bridge and the castle.

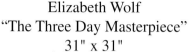

Elizabeth Wolf
"The Three Day Masterpiece"
31" x 31"

["Lizzy" was one of the valiant "pinch-hitters" who bravely took on one of the manhole cover designs late in the game. Receiving the design in the mail three days before my original deadline, she set to work with an enviable tenacity. – Shirley]

"I took 2 jars of peanut butter, a box of raisins, and enough tea for three days down to my sewing studio, outside my home. There I camped, coming home to sleep a few hours, only to get up and immediately return to my work. By the third day, my "um-pa-pa" was flagging. I was so tired that I fell asleep at the sewing machine while my foot was still on the pedal!" In her interpretation of Iwakuni City's manhole cover design, she uses "mostly silk for the background, with the rest, mostly velvet. The sky and sun are tie-dyed silks."

"I live alone on a mountainside in Arkansas, with my dog, and spend most of my time gardening, painting, sewing, or walking. I care about the earth, I grow my own food, I recycle everything - usually into some form of practical art. I enjoy a few friends and travel whenever I can. Silks, velvets, and brocades are my favorite fabrics…, Bright colored threads - variegated, metallic, and knotted - give me a palette from which I can draw beautiful scenes of lakes, people, animals and flowers…"

松戸市

Matsudo City

Matsudo city is located in north Chiba Prefecture, about 20 km from downtown Tokyo. It has a population of 460,000, which makes it a fairly large city by western standards.

One of the city's most significant attractions is the historic Hondo-ji, a temple constructed in 1227. The park-like grounds of the temple feature 30,000 hydrangeas in a variety of colors, which blossom in late June.

The Yagiri Ferry, which has been used as the theme of the Matsudo manhole cover design, has been transporting passengers across the Edo river to Tokyo (formerly Edo) for the past 380 years.

Matsudo offers another spectacular floral display, which is found on its Sakura-dori (cherry street). This is a virtual tunnel of 700 flowering cherry trees that come to their full splendor each year in early April.

Matsudo has a longstanding sister-city relationship with Whitehorse, Victoria, Australia.

Marion Connaughton "The Fun Ferry" 21.5" x 22"

"Fabrics used are 100% cotton. The water was cut in 2 inch squares from a larger print and fused onto fabric as a background. The skyline was cut out in one piece and fused, also. I did machine piecing, fusing, hand and machine appliqué, machine embroidery embellishing and highlighting, and hand embroidery. As I was working with a deadline to meet, I had to keep panic in check and work slowly and carefully and pray for no goofs! Fortunately there were no disasters — just near misses. I still feel that divine intervention had a little hand in the successful completion of my project." *[Hmmm, perhaps it did. When one of the designs "bounced back" on very short notice, Marion appeared on the horizon! – Shirley]*

Marion lives in Chula Vista, near San Diego, Calilfornia. She is a nurse by profession, a friend to animals – especially cats – and, of course a quilter. "Being widowed, I do a lot of volunteer work in animal welfare and other community organizations. My hobbies are cats, quilts (often cat related) and computers." Part of Marion's work has been with Quilt Visions-San Diego, where she has served in a number of capacities, and most recently as a board member.

Matsumoto City

松本市

Here is a city well worth a visit. Located in one of Japan's most beautiful regions, Matsumoto – The Mountain City – is nestled in what is termed the "Japanese Alps," and rests beneath snowcapped 9,000 foot peaks in scenic Nagano Prefecture. Although the city has a population of some 200,000, its setting gives it a somewhat rural atmosphere.

Matsumoto is a castle town, whose virtually intact castle is one of only four to be designated national treasures by the Japanese government. Constructed in the late 16th century, this impressive 6-story structure, with its beautiful grounds and striking backdrop of mountain peaks, is indeed unique. Housed within its lower floors is a museum containing period war materials and articles from the castle's long and colorful history.

Matusmoto's Ukiyo-e Museum maintains one of the largest and most impressive collections of woodblock prints in the world. The more than 100,000 items (prints, screens and books) are presented in rotating displays throughout the year.

The city's manhole covers are adorned with decorative ornaments called *temari.* These small spheres date to the 14th century, when they were children's toys made from scraps of fabric and decorated with silk threads from old kimono.

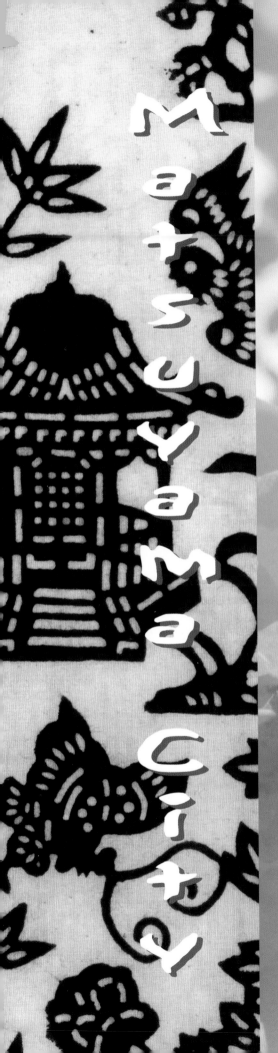

松山市

Matsuyama City, with a population of 430,000 inhabitants, is the largest municipality on the island of Shikoku in Ehime Prefecture. Located on the eastern side of the island, it is three hours by ferry to Hiroshima.

The city has a number of historic sites, but its castle, which rests atop a hill in the center of town, and the ancient Dogo Onsen (hot spring), are its most notable attractions.

Matsuyama-jo (which means "pine mountain castle,") dates from feudal times, and is one of the most well-preserved structures of its kind in Japan. Originally completed in 1603, it has gone through several restorations, the most recent of which was completed in 1986.

Dogo Onsen is said to be 3000 years old, and according to legend was discovered when an injured stork flying low to the steaming pool, dragged his leg in the water and was healed. True or not, the spring has been famous for its health-giving qualities since ancient times. Today, the onsen is housed in a building that dates from 1894, and has become a tourist attraction in its own right.

Another point of interest in Matsuyama City is a museum featuring a unique weaving style native to the area, called Iyo-Kasuri. The resulting product is an attractive indigo-dyed fabric with distinctive patterns.

The manhole cover of Matsuyama features the camellia, the city's flower, which is said to bring hope and happiness to its citizens.

"All of the fabrics used in the quilt are silk. The light purple background is material from a summer kimono. The brown is taken from an obi (a kimono sash). The red is from inside lining of a child's kimono, the green is also kimono material, and the black is taken from a *haori* (a traditional Japanese coat). I used ribbon for the embroidery of the letter and number symbols."

Harumi lives with her husband and family in Zushi City, Kanagawa Prefecture, Japan. She was born in 1926, but started quilting in 1995. "When I made my daughter's first dress, it gave me great joy. Now my pleasure is quilting using old silk fabrics. I am very happy to be participating in the manhole cover project." Harumi is a member of Crazy Quilters.

[Okayama-san was among my first students when I began teaching in Japan – Shirley]
(See Footnote 3)

Harumi Okayama
"Early Spring"
20.25" dia.

Diane Cleland-Boyle
"Dis Manholed"
29" x 39.5"

Diana used cotton, silk organdy, and hand-dyed fabrics for her manhole quilt, and created the design using appliqué, hand piecing, couching and thread painting. "I first envisioned my piece in bronze and silver with a cobble-stone square affect around the cover. The more I played with the design, the more the flowers called for color, and as soon as they got color, they popped out of the rim. They just seemed to want to shine and proclaim!"

"A lifelong seamstress, I began quilting in 1995 with a local charity group for kids." Her quilts have been exhibited in a number of shows in the Pacific Northwest." Diana lives in the Willamette Valley in Oregon, and belongs to a several art-quilt groups in the area.

美祢市

Mine City

Mine (pronounced mee-nay) is located in Yamaguchi Prefecture, at the extreme west end of Honshu. Mine's claim to fame is fossils, of which it has a great many. The city has a museum with a wealth of fossils from various ages. For those unable to visit Mine, there is a "virtual" museum available on the Web. There you will find pictures and information on the area's prehistoric offerings – in English, too! Featured on the site is Dr. Goro Okafuji, whose story is truly inspiring. "Goro-chan" (little Goro) was a native of Mine who became a teacher, and dedicated his life to studying and teaching about the fossils and other natural phenomena of the area.

As might be expected, Mine's manhole cover has a fossil theme, which features spirals of ammonites.

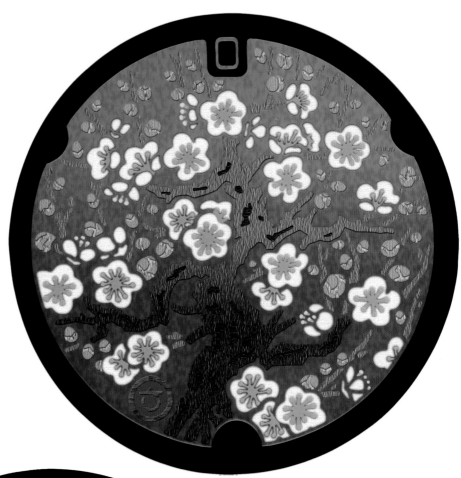

Nagaokakyo City

長岡京市

A custom in feudal Japan was to move the country's capital each time a new emperor came to power. Thus in 784, when Emperor Kanmu assumed control, he selected Nagaokakyo as his seat of government. Alas, its place in the sun was short lived, as just ten years later the center of power was again shifted, this time to Heiankyo (Kyoto), where it remained for over 1,000 years.

Today this city of 78,000, located between Kyoto and Osaka, retains many significant relics of its illustrious past, with tombs, temples and shrines dating far back into Japanese history.

Bamboo has been an important crop in Nagaokakyo for more than three hundred years, and was chosen as the theme of the city's manhole cover.

Judy Northfield
"Dividing Circles"
22.5" x 22.5"

"The quilt is made from 100% cotton. The grey background and some of the other materials within the circle I hand dyed. I used mainly appliqué and reverse appliqué for the central medallion, which was hand stitched, as were the circles. Other shapes within the circle were attached with [fusible] web and machine stitched using a decorative buttonhole stitch. Stained glass appliqué was used to delineate the 'petals' of the 'buds,' using home made bias strips. The quilt was hand stitched "in the ditch." The actual design of the manhole cover was greatly simplified, using only those elements that would stand out when seen from a distance."

Judy lives in Westerfield, Suffolk County, England. "I have always sewn. I started with dolls' clothes, made from scraps given me by a draper who believed in starting sewers young, and progressed to dressmaking. I then dabbled in embroidery, until attending an evening class in patchwork about ten years ago, and became hooked!" Judy has since completed part one of the City and Guilds course in Patchwork and Quilting. (See footnote 2)

長崎市

The name Nagasaki brings some pretty grim images to mind, as well it should. But Nagasaki is a great deal more than a symbol of the dawn of atomic warfare. Two thirds of the city escaped the devastation of the atom bomb, thus many buildings and artifacts of its long and colorful past still remain intact. Although it is not my intention to diminish the importance of what took place there in 1945, I will confine these few comments to Nagasaki's rich cultural heritage, and its role in opening Japan to the West.

The Portuguese arrived in the tiny fishing port of Fukae (now Nagasaki), quite by accident, in 1542, and trade began shortly thereafter. In 1549, Jesuit missionaries appeared on the scene, led by Fr. Frances Xavier (who later attained sainthood). The mission was quite successful, winning many converts to Christianity. Meanwhile, Nagasaki's importance as a trading port grew, ultimately attracting the Dutch, British and Spanish, and luring Chinese traders from the more established port of Fukuoka. In the next hundred years, the city grew in size, character, and importance, finally becoming the most successful port in Kyushu Prefecture, and a center of Western culture and religion.

As one might imagine, such developments were looked upon with a wary eye by Japanese rulers. The trend in Nagasaki was clearly western, and the Church of Rome's influence on its citizens steadily increasing. Thus, in the latter part of the 16th century, persecution began against Christians, and grew steadily, finally resulting in the expulsion of foreigners. Two exceptions were the Chinese and the Dutch, who had no political or religious agendas. Their presence was tolerated, but restricted to a small island off the coast. This began Japan's 250-year isolation, which was broken when US Commodore Matthew Perry arrived in Yokohama in 1853, demanding that the Japanese open their ports to trade. When these demands were met, Nagasaki once again rose to prominence as an international trade center.

Today, Nagasaki is a bustling city of 450,000, and still has a rich and varied cultural heritage to share.

The theme of Nagasaki's manhole cover is the city's flower, the hydrangea.

Tamie Kimura
"Purple Rain"
25" x 20.5"

My manhole cover design is that of Nagasaki City. The hydrangea is my favorite flower, so I was very happy to make it. When I began this project, I decided to dye all the fabrics by myself. I felt that the quilt would be more original and more authentic if I used some very old dyeing techniques. In making this quilt, I dyed silk and linen fabrics, using *katazome* (a kind of stencil dyeing using natural colors) and *shibori* (tie-dyeing, using traditional Japanese blue coloring).

Tamie lives with her family in Yokosuka, Japan, in a wonderful old and traditional Japanese house. "I volunteer as a teacher of Japanese to foreigners, which is where I met Shirley MacGregor. I have been quilting for 15 years. When I saw the TV drama 'Little House on the Prairie,' I was impressed with the many quilts used, and decided that, when I had children, I would make quilts for them. And I have been quilting ever since." (See footnote 3 & 5)

Shirley MacGregor
"Uncommon Will"
29.5" x 25"

This quilt was made using a fabric similar to ultra suede. I wanted to use the cover design without changing it, though not wanting to have it look like a manhole cover, yet it is still there if you look closely. I also took the flowers outside of the cover.

60

名古屋市

Nagoya is Japan's fourth largest city, with a population of over two million. It is also home to one of the country's largest industrial zones. Nagoya suffered extensive damage during World War II, but has been reconstructed with sound planning and foresight.

The city grew up around Nagoya-jo, a castle built in the early 1600's by Tokugawa Ieyasu. The structure, which also sustained heavy war damage, was carefully reconstructed in 1959. Its museum displays an impressive collection of relics from feudal times. Gracing the roof of the castle are two large, heavily gilded dolphin-like sea animals.

Many treasures from the illustrious Tokugawa family remain in Nagoya at the Tokugawa Art Museum, and the Hosa Library. The former exhibits a formidable collection treasures from the Edo period, and the latter holds a priceless collection of ancient books, some of which are national treasures.

There are two Nagoya manhole covers shown here. One depicts the city's symbols and attributes, and the other, a whimsical water spider. The former is based upon the *maru-hachi* (circle-eight). The two birds replace the similar-looking character representing the number 8). Other circles in the design portray significant features of the city, and its symbolic flower, the lily.

The second manhole cover design shows a smiling water spider looking down through the ripples of the water upon which he rests. Perhaps he is peering down at his victim!

NAGOYA

Cindy Sisler Simms
35" x 38"

"With Nagoya City, I started with a light blue cotton with glitter as the background, which I used to represent water… I found a black knit, again with glitter, to give the silhouettes some depth. And because I used a plain solid black as the outside ring, I decided to use gold tissue lamé for the circles surrounding each silhouette. Then, with the horseshoe-shaped half circle connecting the other circles, I used a bronze color tissue lamé. I brought in red using it sparingly in the flowers around the outside edge as well as the thin circle around the center birds. Because the flowers were on the top outer edge, I used red for the letters in the outside black circle to help balance the whole piece. I used machine quilting with mono-filament thread."

"I was raised in the Appalachian Mountains in Western Maryland, where my love of quilting started when both grandmothers taught me to quilt, starting at age 5. I excelled in quilting so that by age 10 I had made my first full-size quilt, all by hand." Cindy lives in Woodbridge, Virginia. She teaches quilting and conducts workshops in the Southeast. (See footnote 1)

Naha City

那覇市

The 57 islands that comprise Okinawa Pre-fecture are different from the rest of Japan, not only physically, but historically and philosophi-cally. Called the Kingdom of Ryukyu until rela-tively recent times, the population aligned itself more closely with the China than with Japan. Today, Okinawans remain very independent in their thinking and in many of their customs.

The Ryukyu kingdom carried on trade with mainland China, Southeast Asian countries, as well as with Japan and Korea. These influences, along with the tropical climate and available resources, have made Okinawan textiles truly unique. Among these is *Bashofu*, which is made from the stalks of a non-fruit-bearing banana tree. Threads are stripped from the stalks of this plant and woven into a loose fabric suited to the warm, tropical climate. Other processes, such as Shuri-ori weaving – which developed under the influences of Okinawa's southeast Asian neighbors – and *Bingata* – a fabric-painting method employing bright colors and traditional designs – are enjoying renewed popularity. De-mand for these unique textiles for use in kimono has increased sharply in recent years.

Naha is Okinawa's major city. Its man-hole cover design was the inspiration of Mr. Yasuhiro Niyagi, and features rings of small fish chasing each other with open mouths. The sym-bol of Naha City rests in the center.

Nancy Hawkins   25" x 34"   Eugene, Oregon

"I started this fish quilt at Camp Quilt Patch near Eugene, Oregon when I took a class in Quilting with Manhole Covers from Shirley MacGregor in the summer of 1999.

At first, the pattern seemed a bit daunting even to trace, but I was intrigued with the idea of doing a cut-out design and putting color behind the cut-out windows. Tracing the design on the grey and black Japanese style wave fabric and cutting out all the separate fish shapes was tedious. However the fun came in playing with the colors behind the cut-outs. My friends all got into the act (when I let them) and all the bright batiks I had brought to camp were wonderful to put together to fill the spaces. I satin stitched around each fish with vibrant rayon threads... another labor of love...

The manhole cover containing its smaller and smaller fish appears to be spinning downstream on the falling water surrounded by larger fish, while dragonflies continue the circular motion overhead."

Sheila Steers
"Seafood Variations"
57" x 23"

"I had the design for a long time and did not do anything with it because I didn't like the direction the concepts were taking me. When I hit upon the idea of taking a less serious approach, it took about 2 days to get the wave background finished. The quilt is machine pieced and quilted, with the beading of the fish eyes the only handwork. After cutting out the spaces between the fish I fused the fabric to the blue background. The wheel is covered with a multi-colored silk chiffon and then each fish was outlined with transparent nylon thread. The fish wheel is actually a separate little quilt attached to the wave background. Once I got over the need to be serious about making this design I had a lot of fun adding the sushi dishes. The sushi print is covered with a white chiffon and sewn down with an iridescent thread."

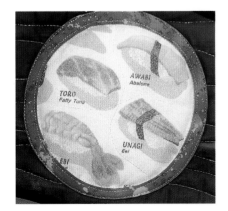

"I have been quilting for almost 25 years. I find my life increasingly involved with different aspects of quilting, from the fabrics, ideas, processes, and planning while moving between the traditional and contemporary styles. Through quilting, I have traveled, made friends, learned new techniques and found good places to eat."

Sheila lives in the Willamete Valley, in Oregon. (see footnote 1)

Signature on back of quilt

69

Nakatsu City

中津市

Nakatsu, a municipality with 70,000 inhabitants, is located in the extreme northeast of the island of Kyushu, in Oita Prefecture. The city developed around a castle constructed by Yoshitaka Kuroda in 1587, on land he received in recognition of a successful campaign against a rival clan.

Nakatsu was also the home of Yukichi Fukuzawa, born in 1834 and destined to become the city's most illustrious citizen.

When Fukuzawa was just 19 years old, he developed an interest in the Dutch language. By 23, he had opened a school to teach his newly-acquired tongue. In later years, he founded Keio University, and lead the first official fact-finding mission to the US. Through his studies and scholarly writings, he was instrumental in bringing an understanding of Western countries and cultures to Japan for the first time. This was to have a profound affect on the country's political growth. In recognition of his contribution, his image appears on Japan's ¥10,000 note.

Usa, a community just to the east of Nakatsu, gained notoriety after WWII when Japanese industries – whose products were of questionable quality – supposedly registered their companies in Usa, enabling them to legitimately use the term, "Made in USA."

The central theme of Nakatsu's manhole cover is its castle, with boatsmen carrying goods in the foreground.

Yuki Fushiki
"Clean"
39" x 41"

"For this quilt, I used cotton material – both Japanese and American. The quilt is hand pieced and hand appliquéd. I tried to use yellow as much as possible, as it is my favorite color."

Yuki lives in Kawasaki City, near Yokohama, in Japan. An

accomplished quilt artist and teacher, she began quilting in 1986. She is a member of the Japan Handicraft Instructors Association, and the Crazy Quilters – a group for sharing and discussion – which meets in nearby Yokosuka City. Her quilts have been shown in Japan and in the United States. (See footnote 3 & 5)

奈良市

Nara City

Nara fits nicely into the "best-kept-secrets" category of many guidebooks on Japan. It does not have the mystique and stature of nearby Kyoto, but historically it is just about as significant. The city served briefly as the seat of government beginning in 710AD, and played an important role in shaping the character and culture of Japan. As Kyoto moved into the forefront of political and cultural life, Nara diminished in proportion. This has been beneficial, however, as many of the relics of its former prominence remain intact.

Today, this city of 350,000 has a great deal to offer the visitor, from unparalleled cultural treasures to beautiful natural surroundings. Todai-ji temple, one of many ancient temples and shrines to be found in Nara, is the world's largest wooden structure. It houses the Great Buddha, a 48-foot-tall, 500-ton bronze statue cast in the mid-8th century. Nara Koen, the city's beautiful park, measures some 8 km square, and is home to approximately a thousand deer. The deer are depicted in the Nara manhole cover, along with the city symbol, the "eight-fold cherry blossoms of old Nara City," made famous in a song from the Heian period (8th to 12th century).

Diane Overman
"Nature's Beauty"
18" dia.

Dianne's manhole cover creation is machine appliquéd with batiks, florals, and "whatever I had on hand. I used the book, *Fantasies & Flowers*, by Kumiko Sudo, for the flowers. The background is a light gray/white leaf print. I had a hard time deciding what flowers to use to represent the city. I thank Kris Bishop for mentoring me on this project." [see page 122]

Diane lives in Woodbridge, Virginia, with her husband and two teenagers. She began quilting in 1995, and enjoys hand and machine quilting, and making both wall and bed-size quilts. "I quilt every minute I can."

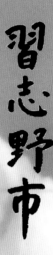

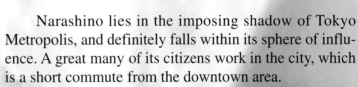

Narashino lies in the imposing shadow of Tokyo Metropolis, and definitely falls within its sphere of influence. A great many of its citizens work in the city, which is a short commute from the downtown area.

The remarkable feature of Narashino is a 40 hectare (just under 100 acre) mud flat. Tatsu Tidal Flat, by name, it is home to the Yatsu-higata Nature Observation Center, essentially a bird sanctuary. It is remarkable because it exists in this highly developed, industrial/residential complex, where land values are truly astronomical, and pressures to develop the area have been relentless.

Yatsu-higata has been designated a Ramsar Convention site, which means that it is an internationally recognized wetland, and has a fair chance at survival. Still, maintaining such a site so close to a massive urban area has been a daunting enterprise. The naturalists who rescued it, and the city fathers of Narashino, should be commended for their efforts to preserve this unique nature study and recreation center.

I would be remiss if I failed to mention Saburo Saito, who lived in Yatsu when it was a tiny fishing village. In 1974 Mr. Saito came upon a newspaper article telling of efforts to preserve the area. He returned to find it a virtual garbage dump. For a number of years after this discovery, he spent a great deal of his spare time and effort trying to restore the flat to its natural state, and to get others involved in the project. His spirit and determination were instrumental in the preservation of Yatsu-higata.

Narashino has three intriguing manhole cover designs. They are unique not only in their artistic interpretation, but in the fact that they are all square! Thanks to Yoji Inoue of Tokyo, I was able to include the unique designs he created for the city manhole covers.

Barbara Johnson
"Fish"
27" x 26"

Having never before seen a square man-hole cover, I found the Narashino Fish an astounding pattern." Barbara interpreted the design using hand-painted and commercial fabrics, to which she applied metallic, tinsel, and embroidery threads. Added in the mix was, "…a certain amount of blood, sweat, and frustration. (Okay, so I never actually cried)."

A retired nurse, Barbara lives in Fayetteville, Arkansas. "I stitched my first quilt when I was six years old to cover my doll; now, all my family, and most of my friends sleep under my quilts. I believe if you have a creative statement to make, you will find a medium through which to express yourself; my medium is fabric and thread."

Betty Buckly
"Under The Sea"
32.5" x 32.5"

[Of all the quilts that arrived here in Korea for the photo shoot, none pleased me more than Betty's. After she carefully placed it in the mail, it went missing for over two months. We finally came to the conclusion that it had been permanently lost or stolen. With emotions going from anxiety to despair, Betty finally initiated a claim with the US Postal Service. She had taken some fairly good digital pictures before sending it off, so we were prepared to use those for the book. Joy returned when the package was discovered on a shelf at our post office – where it had been sitting all the time! – Shirley]

To design her manhole cover quilt, Betty "visited 17 Internet web sites about squid showing pictures of almost all the varieties. Extremely interesting, and information which helped me do my squid. I used mainly cotton fabric for the quilt, but did use silk for the four crabs, and Ultrasuede™ for the squids' eyes." She used a variety of interesting threads in her design, and used iridescent, sparkling cord on the crab legs.

Betty lives with her family in Fayetteville, Arkansas. She has been quilting since 1986, and has taught classes at quilt shops and guilds in the area. "My love right now tends to be reverse appliqué. I love handwork of all kinds because it is soothing and keeps stress down. Music, laughter, and people are always in my life." Describing herself, she borrows a sentiment from Will Rogers, claiming that she never met a person she didn't like, admitting that sometimes it is necessary to dig well beneath the surface before striking the human equivalent of gold.

Christina Brown
"Narashino"
"38" x 39.5"

   "The first, second and thirtieth look at this whimsical design all said 'appliqué' to me as the method of construction. I decided to take an organic approach to the shapes, and use batiks, hand-dyed fabrics, some iridescent synthetics and Ultrasuede™ as a means of expressing color and textures."
   Christina was raised and educated in Chicago, but eventually migrated to the Pacific Northwest, where she has been engaged in quilting for "a short but intense time…." She holds a degree in Fine Arts, and over the years, has applied her talents to a wide range of activities. "[I'm] always in the process of creating something, be it art, quilts, clothes, stuffed animals, jewelry, gardens, web sites, design projects, or dinner."
   [Note: Christina created The Carriage Trade Press site, www.carriagetradepress.com]

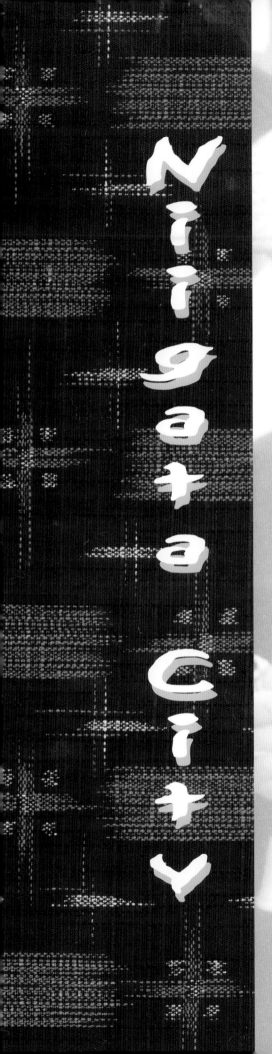

新潟市

Niigata City

Niigata is a large city of nearly a half million located on the western coast of Honshu, Japan's main island. The capital of Niigata Prefecture, it is a major industrial center, and a hub of transportation and commerce. Niigata was one of the five ports which were opened to trade from the West subsequent to Commodore Perry's arrival in the early 1850's. It remains one of Japan's major gateways.

In this book you will find representations of six of Niigata's seven manhole cover designs.

Mi-Oak Kwon
"Love Environment"
67" x 36.5"

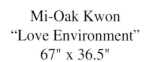

"In creating my quilt, I looked at the manhole cover as a mediating element, covering the polluted water on its way to purification. In a way it is like a transition point between the underground root of a plant and its leaf. To express this concept, I took the design, divided it in half, and "planted" a garden between the two parts. Look closely and you will see many interesting plants and animals growing in the good, clean environment of the garden."

Mi Oak Kwon lives in Seoul, South Korea. She is a graduate of Seoul Women's University, with a major in Visual Design. As a quilter, she prefers hand appliqué, and likes to express the inspiration she derives from nature. (See footnote 4)

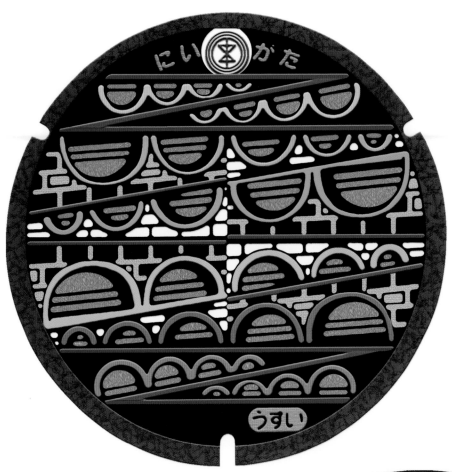

Barbara Eikmeier
"The Wishing Box"
31.5" x 45.5"

"I had a design drawn out, but was having problems figuring out how to construct the quilt. I spent a morning pondering the situation when I decided to go back to the original design. When I looked at it again I suddenly saw it as a hinged sphere, which totally changed my idea for the quilt." Barbara used cotton fabrics which she machine and hand appliquéd using the mola – or reverse-appliqué – technique. She applied three-dimensional flowers with a small amount of stuffed work and employed machine quilting.

Barbara was raised on a dairy farm in northern California. Married to a career army officer, she has had the opportunity to live in many locations including Seoul, South Korea, where she met the author. She has been quilting since 1984 and teaching quilting to adults and children since 1990. "Although I consider myself a traditionalist, I have a great fascination with the fabric manipulations of contemporary quilt artists. Appliqué is my favorite, and I enjoy exploring both machine and hand-appliqué techniques." Barbara has authored three books on quilting. (See footnote 4)

Haruyo Yamada
"Four Moods"
20" dia.

Haruyo Yamada used all cotton fabrics and reverse appliqué for this interesting Niigata manhole cover. She was very faithful to the original concept, leaving little holes where the real manhole cover is notched for lifting purposes. She used a variety of interesting colors to make the design come alive. The design represents four moods, and if you look closely, you can see representations of happiness, sadness, anger and surprise .

Haruyo lives in Hayama, a picturesque coastal town not far from Yokohama. She is married with grown children, and has traveled extensively throughout the world. She began quilting in 1985, and is a Nihon Vogue-certified teacher and lecturer in quilting. She has attended lectures in America, France, England, Austria and Australia. "It has been interesting to meet lecturers from many different countries, "she says, "…I have learned a great deal from them." Haruyo is a member of the Crazy Quilters. (See footnote 3 & 5)

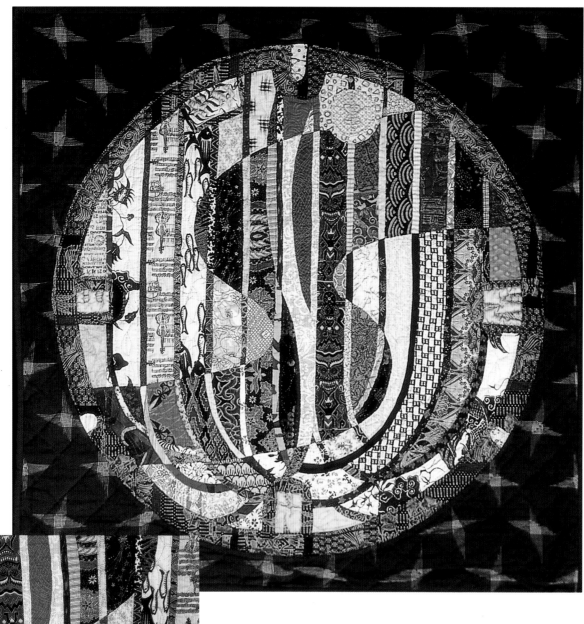

Madelaine Hutchin
"Forest Afloat"
34" x 34"

"I wanted to use a great variety of fabrics and actually managed Dutch shirting, Indonesian batik, Maltese, African and Indian fabrics together with Liberty™ and American pieces." The quilt was hand pieced and hand and machine quilted, with variegated gold metallic thread. Madelaine used touches of gold paint to embellish the piece. "'Forest Afloat' was my husband's chosen name for the quilt, which seemed to fit. He has always given me great names for all my quilts."

Madelaine and her husband Charles presently live in Sussex, in the south of England, but over the years have lived in Africa, the Middle East, and Asia. She has been quilting for over 20 years, has studied with City and Guilds, taught patchwork at a local college, and has had her work displayed at numerous locations in the UK. She specializes in eastern fabrics, particularly silks and batiks. (See footnote 1)

Mary Goodson
"Short Tree"
30" x 22.5"

Mary was taken by the complexity of this Niigata design, and decided to translate it faithfully to cloth. "I chose to do the entire piece in silks that are subtle in color to keep the emphasis on the design." The river was appliquéd and machine quilted. She used hand-painted silk <u>dupioni</u> for the trunk of the tree and branches, which she hand appliquéd, then added machine quilting around these features to give it dimension. She free-form quilted the piece, and attached the leaves with beads.

Inspired by an artist neighbor as a child, Mary received a BA in Design, with an emphasis on Fiber Art. Her pieces have hung in galleries and juried shows throughout the Northwest. Mary lives with her husband in Eugene, Oregon.

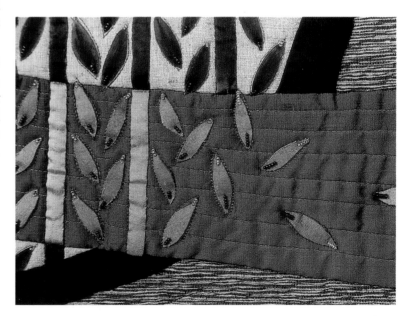

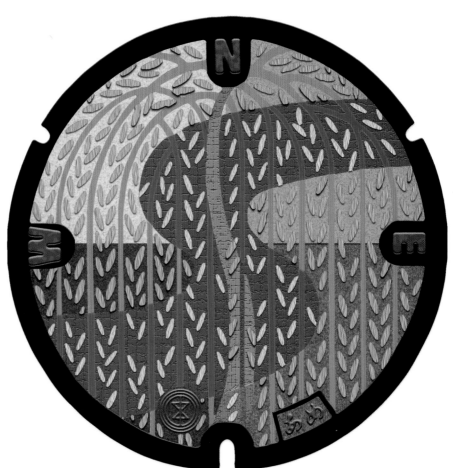

Terry Snitger
"Indigo Sky"
32" x 29"

"For this quilt, I used fabrics I acquired while living in Japan. My passion is indigo blue fabrics which are the base of this manhole project. The curved lines of my pattern were a problem at the outset, but I solved this dilemma through sashiko. The white on blue contrast effectively transfers the detail of the design. I toyed with trying to stencil the Japanese characters, but was voted down by my family of critics. They were right and it looks better stitched. Fortunately, my Japanese friends were able to provide the sashiko thread I was in desperate need of, and act as a sounding board for my ideas. Using beads and sequins enhanced the basic style and added texture. The border is a sampling of my collection of Japanese indigo fabrics and patterns."

"I have been quilting off and on for 19 years. I like to machine piece and hand quilt. My quilting desire was reborn in Japan where I worked with American and Japanese quilters. Working with Japanese fabrics and techniques is my new passion." Terry now lives in Santa Fe, New Mexico, where she and her husband operate a camping facility. (See footnote 3)

Glenda Beasley
"Life is to Short to Appliqué"
28.75" x 28.75"

"The quilt is mostly cotton, with a small amount of shiny, slippery satin, and some unidentified stretchy, sparkly stuff." Frustrated after three attempts at a troublesome seagull, Glenda mentions, "That bird was a real pain. I lived with the first one for about a week, but he just didn't grow on me. When I looked at the quilt, it looked like a clunky bird, with some stuff in the background. …I [thought] perhaps he would look better with an eyeball, but I only had white and red beads." Eventually accepting her effort at avian art, she notes that "…a bird on the quilt is worth two in the trash pile."

A good friend, and sage advisor in a number of areas, Glenda is currently tucked away in Doha, Qatar, in the Middle East. A military spouse, Glenda has carried her passion for quilting, and her formidable and ever-growing stash of fabrics to the far corners of the earth. "The last hurdle will be naming it. I can think of some, but they seem a little trite. How about 'A Bird on the Quilt...' or 'Life is Too Short to Appliqué' Or 'Gone Fishing' (do seagulls eat fish?) Or 'The Bird…' Although pleased with the results, she is still inclined to say that 'Life is Too Short to Appliqué.'"

小樽市

Otaru City

Otaru is an old port city located on Japan's northern island of Hokkaido, just to the northeast of Sapporo City. Once a major center for trade with the mainland, such activity has diminished since the mid-1900's. Today, Otaru's primary port activity is ferrying passengers to points along the Japanese coast and to a few ports in Siberia. The harbor area still retains a good measure of charm from its glory days, however. Many of the 19th century western-style buildings fronting on the city's picturesque canal have been restored and are being used for more modern commerce. The two sea otters pictured on Otaru's manhole cover are favorites at the city's aquarium.

"The Rising Otter Earth is observed from the moon by the first Cat Astronauts. NCASA on the space suits stands for National Cat Aero Space Administration." In producing his quilt, Paul "utilized fabric that I painted with transparent Setacolors™. The fabric is high-count, mercerized cotton, which is rather difficult to hand quilt…. The fabrics, with the exception of the borders, are painted to look like skies with clouds. The universe, with nebulae, stars and other things seen with a telescope, are material painted to look like the surface of the moon. I used two commercial blue cotton fabrics in the borders.

In response to the question of any problems along the way, Paul says, "Madness! Doing reverse appliqué and finding myself trying to turn under four threads!"

Paul Wank
"Otter Earth Rising"
35.5" x 47"

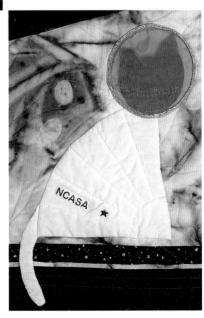

Paul, a retired librarian, lives in Eurika Springs, Arkansas. He is a cat lover, which is evident in his manhole cover design. "I try to have a cat or two somewhere in the quilts I make." He took up quilting to utilize the fruits of his labor as a fiber artist. "I became interested in weaving and spinning and making my own fabric using cottons, flax, wool and silk fibers. The logical extension of this is, of course, is using my created fabrics. I have been quilting since 1985."

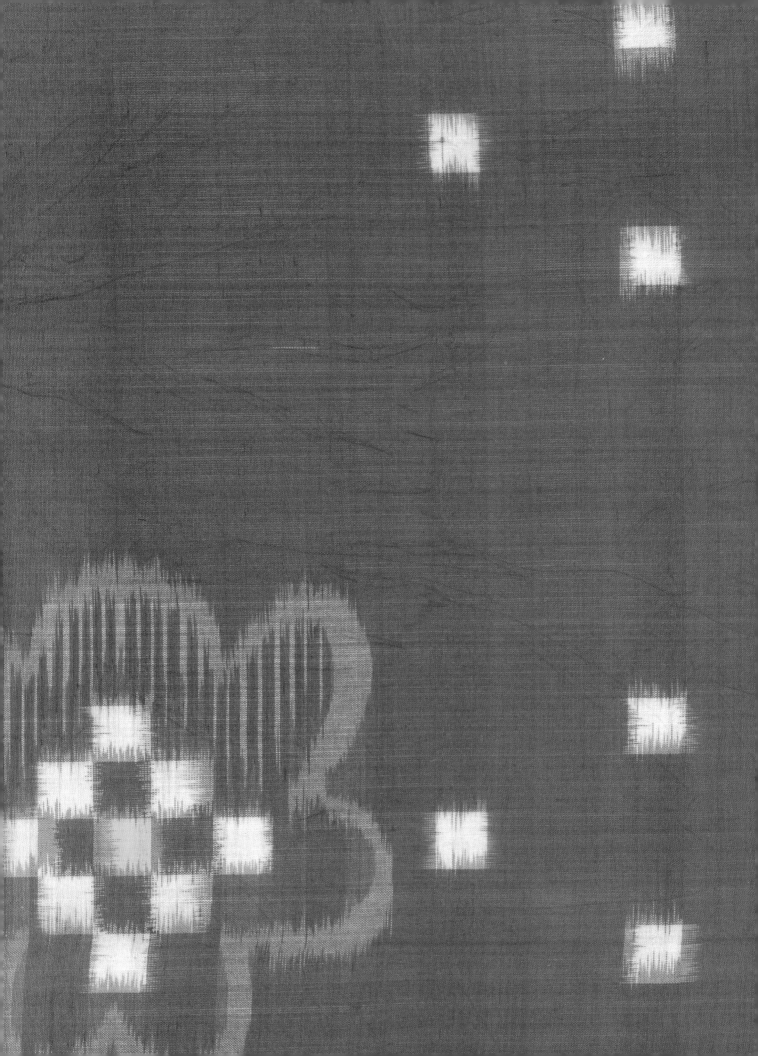

Otsu City

大津市

Historic Otsu city is located at the southern tip of the Biwa-ko, Japan's largest fresh-water lake. Now capitol of Shiga Prefecture, Otsu was for a brief period the capitol of Japan. It was one of the principal cities along the Tokaido Road between Kyoto and Edo (Tokyo), and its many significant shrines and temples stand in testimony to its importance in Japan's history.

Among the many attractions to be found in Otsu are the remains of Azushi Castle. The castle was built by warlord Oda Noburaga in the 16th century as a base for his ambitious attempt to unify the many warring factions in Japan. Today, an archeological museum rests on the site and offers glimpses into this fascinating period in Japanese history.

Just a few kilometers to the north of Otsu is another noteworthy attraction; the Enryaku-ji Temple. It was founded in 788 by Saicho, a rather remarkable Buddhist priest who stands among the most significant of Japan's religious leaders.

In its heyday, the temple boasted a great many buildings and a thousand or so *sohei*, or warrior monks. It became such a threat to the ruling faction that it was attacked and burned, with nearly all of its many buildings destroyed, and its inhabitants killed.

Today, Otsu is a thriving city of 290,000 people, with throngs of tourists replacing the pilgrims who gathered there in times past.

Lynne Ackerman, Nancy Hawkins
and Nancy Naishtat
"Otsu 1000"
36.5" x 54.5"

The Otsu quilt features a variety of machine and hand-appliqué techniques using batiks. Each quilter took on various aspects of the design, hoping that "…divine intervention would bring the individual elements into a coherent whole." And it worked!

Here are three quilters who have "joined hands" to create a beautifully detailed work representing Otsu City. Lynne Ackerman, Nancy Hawkins, and Nancy Naishstat, who live in the Eugene, Oregon, began their "conspiratorial" efforts on a project to raise money for the American Cancer Relay for Life, and found that they enjoyed this team approach to quilting. Co-workers at a local hospital, they … "share the love of the outdoors and have had fun times sewing in lovely settings like the Oregon coast and the Cascade Mountains."

Bunnie Jordan
"2000 Otsu City"
23" x 46.5"

"For this project, I used Oriental cotton fabrics. The piece is appliquéd and machine quilted. As with the other two manhole covers I made, this one is in the form of a hanging scroll. At first, I was intimidated by this design, perhaps because of the people. Time constraints pushed me to take advantage of printed fabrics with the characters represented instead of constructing the elements from scratch. I've been playing with circular designs lately and they worked their way into this piece. Overall size is always a dilemma because I don't have a formula or specific size in mind when I start. I add some borders and keep trying until I feel it's a proportion I'm comfortable with."

Bunnie is a nurse and lives in Vienna, Virginia. She is a quilt appraiser, a board member of the American Quilt Study Group, a teacher at the Jinny Beyer Hilton Head Seminar, and is active in a number of quilting organizations, including American Quilters Society, and the Studio Art Quilt Association. A fan of Oriental design and fabrics, she has been quilting and collecting antique quilts since the early 80's. (See footnote 1)

Otsu City

Terri Willett
"Otsu Sunset"
23" x 23"

Terri's Otsu City design is composed of 100% cotton fabrics. It is hand appliquéd, with the majority of the layers done in reverse appliqué, and machine quilted. "I tried to convey the impression of a sunset over the water, and really struggled to pick the blues. I wanted some contrast, but also wanted the water feeling to come across. I spent many hours "auditioning" fabrics for this top. Once I made up my mind, I'd sew one layer, then change my mind about the next. This quilt was a learning experience for me, and a very enjoyable one."

"I have been sewing since I was a child, but started quilting about 16 years ago, and now specialize in appliqué." Terri is a registered nurse, and lives with her family in Fairfax, Virginia. Her work has appeared in a number of books and magazines, and she teaches locally, and has taught at the Jinny Beyer Hilton Head Seminars for the past six years.

高松市

Takamatsu City

Takamatsu is situated on Shikoku, one of Japan's main islands. It is a port town on the Inland Sea, providing sea links to a number of ports on the main island. Takamatsu is also castle town, and historically significant as the stronghold of various warring factions of centuries past. Notable among such conflicts is a fierce struggle that took place between the Heike and Genji clans in the last half of the 12th century. In a decisive battle, the invading Genji feigned an attack by sea, while setting horsemen ashore to outflank the superior Heike forces. The Takamatsu manhole cover design depicts a Genji warrior who reputedly shot the fan from the hand of a Heike woman during the attack.

TSURUOKA CITY

Tsuruoka is located in Yamagata Prefecture, far up in the northwest corner of Honshu. An old castle town with an interesting history, Tsuruoka has for many years been a stopping place for pilgrims on their way to the Dewa Sanzan, a collective term for three sacred mountains. The mountains – Haguro-san, Gas-san, and Yudono-san – lie within the Bandai-Asahi National Park, and are home to an ascetic Bhuddist-Shinto cult of yamabushi (wandering monks). Some of the finest rice in Japan comes from farms in the Tsuruoka area.

Tsuruoka library, built in 1915, is pictured on its manhole cover, along with its symbols, the cherry blossom and the crane.

Harumi Iida
"Spring Message"
30" x 33.5"

"I selected Tsuruuka for the subject of my manhole quilt because my oldest and best friend lives there. I found it a very frustrating subject, and had difficulty coming up with a good plan. After many annoyances, I went to a fabric shop and found a fabric which I used for the base, as well as some good ideas. I ended up using Japanese cotton fabrics and cotton organdy. I used various appliqué methods – stained glass appliqué and reversed appliqué."

"I was born and raised in the Yokohama area. When I first visited the United States in 1977, I saw an old American stamp quilt in a lighthouse in San Diego. I was fascinated with the quilt, as it looked like something my mother had made. The memory stayed with me through the years, and provided me an interest in quilting, which I began in 1990. I am now a quilting teacher." (See footnote 3 & 5)

四日市市

The name Yokkaichi means "fourth-day market," based on a designation of market days set back in the 1500's. Following its tradition, present-day Yokkaichi has markets in 16 locations spread throughout the city. Located near the geographical center of the country in Mie Prefecture, Yokkaichi was a stop on the Tokaido Road. Shipping has been an important industry in Yokkaichi since its port opened for business in 1899, and the city remains an important container port today. Its textile industry dates from the Meiji period (1868-1912).

Two of the city's three manhole cover designs are represented here. One depicts Yokkaichi's sister-city relationships with Long Beach , California, Sydney, Australia, and Tianjin, China, and the other, the salvia, Yokkaichi's flower.

Kris Bishop
20" x 25.5"

Kris used cottons and lamés for her manhole cover quilt. She employed some new fusing methods, quilted it by hand and machine, and appliquéd it on a larger rectangular background. "[This was] my first big adventure in beading on a quilt." She used her computer and printer to design and print the city's name.

Kris Bishop lives in Woodbridge, Virginia. She brings a great deal of quilting experience and prior knowledge of the "manhole cover genre," to her creation of the Yakkaichi design. "I have been quilting for about forty years, but had a brief break in the 70's while I was overseas. I enjoy both art and traditional quilts, and hand and machine quilting. In other words, I enjoy all aspects of quilting." (See footnote1)

Back art and label

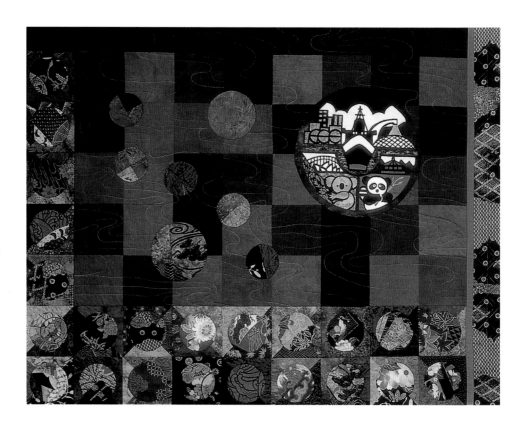

Gay McNeal
"It's A Small World"
58" x 47"

"The quilt is machine pieced, hand and machine appliquéd. It was a challenge as this is the first time I have ever done any real appliqué work. Nothing like trying out a new recipe on dinner guests. I do that too!! I had several false starts deciding how best to proceed. As a result I employed some airbrush/stencil techniques where I felt the appliqué was beyond my skill level. I used a variety of commercial fabrics from my stash and combined them with some fabrics from some of my favorite hand dyers."

Gay lives in Long Beach, California. "I have been actively interested in quilting for about 12 years, but I have always been interested in the fiber arts. In college I was an Interior Design major, but took enough classes in Surface Design and Weaving to be a Textiles major." She is "… partial to art quilts and quilts that push the techniques of traditional quilts." Gay has a specialty textile business, and travels to fiber art shows in California and neighboring states.

[Gay and I ran into each other on the Internet, and after a few message exchanges, discovered that we had quite a bit in common. We both grew up in Long Beach, in the same neighborhood, and attended the same schools. But there's more! When I sent her the Yokkaichi design, it never dawned on me that the ship depicted on the manhole cover is the Queen Mary – now a museum permanently docked in Long Beach. It seems that Yokkaichi and Long Beach are sister cities. – Shirley]

124

山口市

Yamaguchi sits at the eastern tip of Honshu, Japan's main island. It was founded in the 14th century by Hiroyu Ouchi who used the city plan of Kyoto as a model. Through the years, Yamaguchi has developed as a cultural center.

Father (later to become saint) Francis Xavier was welcomed there in 1551, where he converted 500 citizens to Roman Catholicism. The Xavier Memorial Church rests upon a hill on the wooded former site of a Buddhist temple. The site was given to Francis Xavier by Yashitaka Ouchi. Just a year later, however, Yamaguchi was invaded by a rival clan that forced the Ouchi from power and destroyed a large portion of the city.

Several temples and shrines, as well as an ancient hot spring, are worthy of note in Yamaguchi. One of the main attractions, a beautiful five story pagoda, was constructed in 1442 by Hiroyo Ouchi.

Martine House
"Festival of Lights"
27" x 32"

"I find the process of handwork very soothing. So, I use embroidery, appliqué, quilting, or all of these techniques. My pieces are small but very detailed. I like people to come close and discover my world."

For this piece, Martine used 100% cotton fabrics, with a few minor exceptions. It is appliquéd, and reverse appliquéd by hand, with embroidered letters in a hand satin stitch, and is machine quilted. "I put a gold bead on most of the lanterns, just to add a little sparkle."

Martine Caillon-House is a native of France, but now resides in North Carolina. "I come from a family where people made things with their hands: woodwork, knitting, embroidery. They gave me their love for different materials, the need to "touch" things and also the desire to do things as perfectly as I can. Sometimes, that is a curse."

[Martine authored a book on trapunto (available only in France), and publishes Quilt Magazine On Line on the Worldwide Web]

八尾市

Yao City

Located a few kilometers east of metropolitan Osaka, Yao City is an industrial center that has produced a variety of products over the years. During the Edo period, Yao was a major producer of Kawachi cotton, a smooth, simple fabric used for clothing and *"noren,"* or doorway curtains. Demand for Kawachi declined with the introduction of more modern fabrics, and the industry failed. Production of this fabric has seen renewed interest in recent times, however, and has become the theme for the city's manhole cover. Also included in the design is the chrysanthemum, the city's flower, which has been an important agricultural tradition in Yao for many years.

Cindy Sisler Simms
27" x 35"

"I like to experiment with colors and textures, … and use unusual fabrics, embellishments and glitz to create unique quilts. When I first saw [the Yao design], I knew I had to find a fabric in a gold or yellow tone in a print for the background… and a sort of medium small print for the kimono that would look in proportion to the lady, but large enough to stand out against the gold background. Once I found these two fabrics, the rest of the fabrics for this manhole cover seemed to fall in place. From my stash, I pulled a navy cotton with glitter on it for the spinning wheel and used one of my fancy cords in a pink for the thread. I then used different greens with glitz, to give a little more sparkle to the trees and leaves on the outer border."

Cindy lives in Woodbridge, Virginia. She teaches quilting and conducts workshops in the Southeast. (See footnote 1)

Yokosuka City

横須賀市

Yokosuka is a thriving city on Tokyo Bay, 20 km southeast of Yokohama. When Japan opened its doors to the world after 250 years of isolation, Yokosuka began a rapid transition from sleepy fishing village to major ship-building center. The shipyard changed hands in 1945, and has since been home to the US Seventh Fleet. It was my husband's assignment to the American school at Yokosuka Naval Base that brought manhole covers into my life. Yokosuka is also the home of the Crazy Quilters – a dynamic Japanese and American quilting group, several of whose members have produced quilts for this book.

Many examples of "street art" may be found in downtown Yokosuka. Notable among them are life-size people, cast in bronze, sitting pensively on benches along the *ginza* (shopping street). Also, many of the city's utility covers have beautiful designs, some of which shown here.

Marsha Klosterman
27.5" x 31.5"

"When I first saw the manhole pattern, I panicked. All those little pieces! I spent the summer making leaf petals and arranging and rearranging them. The material is mostly cotton, with some lamé for sparkle." While working on the quilt, Marsha wrote, "This quilt has become a group project. It goes with me to my appliqué group every week. My friends have been there every step with advice on design and color. It has brought us closer together and given everyone a bit of ownership."

Marsha lives in Florence, Oregon, and has been quilting since the '70's. "I love all kinds of techniques, especially handwork. Being a Middle School teacher, I love to share my passion with my classes, and have had 6th graders making blocks in the name of geometry.

"Manhole quilts have become a passion because of their unique nature and history."

Hee Ja Lee
27.25" x 38.5"

For this quilt, Hee Ja used a rich floral backing of oriental fabric over which she machine appliquéd the design, embellishing it with beadwork in various areas.

Hee Ja has been quilting for 11 years and is currently teaching at the Dal-Suh Gu community center and So-Sun Women's Middle School. She is president of the quilt division of the Korean Living Craft Association.

[The artist completed her quilt on extremely short notice, graciously agreeing to work on a design which was returned by another quilter – Shirley]

138

Footnotes

Footnote 1: Are quilters that made quilts for my first book "Quilting with Manhole Covers"
Cathy Sperry "Iris in the Road" Miyazaki City
Karen Harmony "We All Live Down Stream" Fujino Town
Cindy Simms Zushi City
Bunnie Jordan "Lotus Blossom" Hasuda City
Sheila Steers "Lillies of Obihiro" Obihiro City and "Fish Ladders" Odawara City
Kris Bishop "Thunderbirds" Fukui City

Footnote 2:City and Guilds in the UK is a part time qualification which comes at two main levels - Part 1 and a more advanced Part 2. You can take it in all sort of creative crafts,e.g. embroidery and lace making.

Footnote 3: A member of Crazy Quilters, a Japanese and American quilting group in Yokosuka City near Yokohama City.

Footnote 4: A member of Happy quilters, a quilting group in Seoul, South Korea.

Footnote 5: Was among the members of a quilt study group, led by the author, that visited guilds and exhibitions in the Pacific Northwest in spring of 1996.

Giantess

The story of the girl who traveled the world in search of freedom.

SCRIPT : J.C. DEVENEY
ART : NURIA TAMARIT

Translation by Dan Christensen
Localization, Editing by Mike Kennedy
Production Assistance and Lettering by Chris Northrop

MAGNETIC™

ISBN: 978-1-951719-61-6
Library of Congress Control Number: 2022906040

Printed in China.

10 9 8 7 6 5 4 3 2 1

Nothing could have prepared the woodcutter for what he discovered that springtime afternoon.

As he usually did, the man had been working since dawn, cutting down trees and preparing the wood for buyers down in the valley.

His work accomplished, he returned to his farm, which was built high on the mountain pastures.

ARF

ARF

And it was then, as he walked along the Great Ravine, that his destiny changed forever.

BUA!

Hiiiiii!

Easy now, Blanche, easy!

Are you all right down there?

BUAAA!

BUAAAAA

Well, now...

It was not uncommon for travelers to lose their way in the night and tumble into the mountain's ravines.

The woodcutter had already provided assistance to many such travelers in the past...

Hang in there! I'm coming!

BUAAAA!

By the Almighty!

...But this time was far different than any other...

Never before had he seen such a large traveler.

Or such a young one, for that matter.

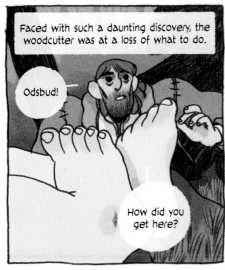

Faced with such a daunting discovery, the woodcutter was at a loss of what to do.

Odsbud!

How did you get here?

For a fleeting moment, he considered retracing his steps and forgetting all of this.

But the man wasn't just a woodcutter.

He was also a father.

DON'T GIVE UP NOW, BLANCHE!

We're almost there!

Ga gueu ga!

Pfft.

Pfft.

Well, I'll be!

At least that put a smile back on your face.

Back in the high pastures, the woodcutter's wife was worried.

The sun had set in the valley and her husband still had not returned.

This wasn't like him.

Something must have happened...

There he is!

Are you all right, Jean?

Not so loud, my wife...

Why... it... it's incredible!

You're telling me! It's the biggest baby I've ever seen!

The most magnificent, you mean! Just look at those chubby cheeks!

Whoa, calm down, my wife! I know what you're up to.

We already have more than enough mouths to feed.

First thing tomorrow, I'm taking him down to the valley.

8

9

Chapter 1
The Six Brothers

The arrival of a new child is always a time of change for a family.

Gueu ga!

It quickly became necessary to increase the size of the herd.

And the changes that Celeste brought with her were proportional to her size.

And to watch over it even more closely.

The vegetable garden grew as well...

Ugk!

...with the baby's digestive process helping considerably.

Luckily, Celeste was an infant who quickly slept all through the night.

ROOONFFL!

RROOONF!

Other steps in her development were not without surprises.

Like her first steps...

BRAOUM!

houiiin!

Her first aesthetic creations...

And the ensuing arguments.

No!

Luckily, her parents were always fair but firm.

HA HA! HA

It should be noted that both of them had experience in this field...

...having already raised six boys with six very different personalities.

Prime, the oldest, was also the calmest.

AOUM

He always did his best to help his parents on the farm and around the house.

Segond was the most spirited, like the horses he raised since he was a child.

A passion he shared with Celeste during her "little pony" period.

Tertio was the most mysterious.

By some strange coincidence, he dreamed only of the ocean...

HA HA!

...and was the first to lead Celeste away from the farm to discover the joys of splashing water.

Quarte was the moodiest.

Stuck between his older and younger brothers, he asserted himself through dangerous challenges...

Let go of me!

...or through terrible fits of anger.

Quintil was the most intelligent.

He had read the rare books found at the farm thousands of times.

It was he who taught Celeste how to read and write...

...thus opening her imagination to a world of knights, queens, and castles.

And finally, there was Sixte, who was also the most fragile.

He would often fall ill and become bedridden. Celeste would then watch over him with the greatest care...

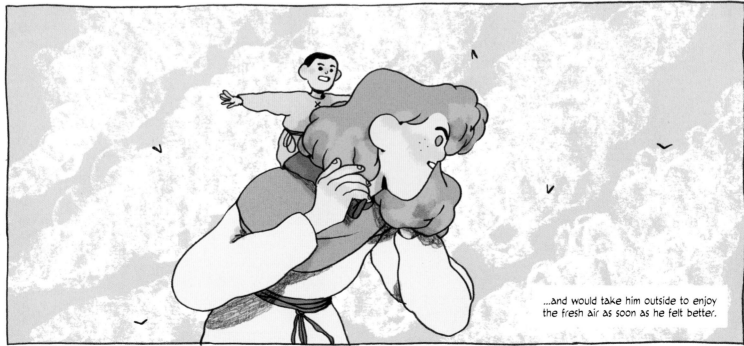
...and would take him outside to enjoy the fresh air as soon as he felt better.

It was thus that Celeste spent her childhood, among her brothers, truly the baby of the family.

They would often ask her for help when they needed her...

...and would exclude her when she would get in their way.

Which could often lead to memorable battles...

...or wonderful escapades...

...with the valley, as always, being their fantasized horizon.

Which soon became a problem.

15

NO! Going with Segond into the valley is out of the question!

But why? All of the boys have already been there! Even Sixte!

Sixte needed to go see a doctor.

Well it just so happens I've caught a cold...

Very funny, Celeste.

I'll keep a low profile, I promise!

Enough! It's not a question of size, but of age.

You are far too young to go exploring in the valley.

So Celeste had to resign herself to letting Segond go to the valley alone.

He returned with enough cloth to make her a new dress...

...and with an announcement that would change their lives forever.

An important livestock farmer asked me to come work for him...

I accepted.

Thus, Segond was the first to leave the family home.

A few months later, it was Tertio's turn to embark upon a merchant vessel.

Prime followed him shortly after, settling down on his own farm nearby.

As for Quintil, the following year he left to become the city printer's apprentice.

With each of these separations, Celeste was torn between feelings of sadness and envy.

But they also brought the three remaining children even closer together.

They're so heavy!

Of course they are! It takes muscle to haul twigs around.

Quit teasing him, Quarte! You know your brother is fragile.

Sixte is in great shape!

I'M NOT FRAGILE!

Come with me, Sixte. You'll help me drive the cart.

But I can carry wood just fine!

And don't question me, please.

Fragile, my eye! Lazy is more like it! Doing nothing is easier than doing chores.

Stop it! You know that's not true!

It's a good thing I'm around! If it wasn't for my strength, nothing would get done.

HA HA!

I love it when you daydream out loud.

CRACK!

What's that? I can cut a tree down faster than you any day!

It's cute that you seem to actually believe that!

Quarte began chopping away with all his might.

CRACK!

Celeste did the same, in her own way.

RRAASS

And although the outcome was close...

Ha ha! Finished!

NiiiEEE

She was the uncontested winner.

Oh, we were only supposed to cut down one?

Pff! I'm sure you started before I did!

Sore loser! Does it hurt to lose to your little sister?

18

Shut up! You're not even my real sister!

What?

You... you're lying!

Our parents found you in some hole in the mountains!

Go on, ask them! You'll see if I'm lying.

Certain revelations in life make you grow up at an alarming speed.

Quarte's words did not diminish the love that Celeste and her parents shared in the slightest.

But they did cause her to ask herself many questions.

Who were her real parents? Were they the same size she was?

Scouring the neighboring hills, she found not the slightest trace of them.

Only the books that Quintil had left behind could offer her insight to her questions...

...for they were filled with marvelous creatures, some of which bore a strange resemblance to her.

The following spring, it was Quarte's turn to leave the farm.

I'm sick of the mountain! I deserve better than this!

Celeste and Sixte were the last children left.

His health had improved, and his brothers' absence had allowed him to become more self-assured...

...even if his parents were not of the same opinion.

BUT WHY DOES HE HAVE TO LEAVE, TOO?

Prime has found an apprenticeship for him with a miller in the valley. The climate down there isn't as harsh. He will feel better there.

But I feel fine right now!

I'm serious! Let me stay! I'll help you with the animals and the wood!

We got by just fine before you children arrived.

But that won't always be the case! With our brothers gone and your advancing age, you're going to need his help.

There's some truth to what Celeste is saying, Jean.

She's interfering with matters that don't concern her!

And I find she's looking down her nose at us a little!

So let's talk about me, then! Why are you keeping me from leaving if I want to?

Celeste, you have no idea how dangerous the world can be for people like you...

People like me?

So it's because of my size that you're keeping me here!

I know I'm different! I'm not stupid!

But my size is the very thing that will keep me safe!

IT HAS NOTHING TO DO WITH YOUR SIZE! YOU'RE A GIRL!

AND YOUR PLACE IS HERE WITH YOUR PARENTS! NOT OUT TRAVELING THE WORLD!

But...?

NOT ANOTHER WORD! THE MATTER IS CLOSED!

Celeste watched as Sixte left, her heart filled with bitterness.

To her, disobeying her parents was inconceivable.

And yet, she could not accept being kept from the outside world.

She never suspected that it would soon be coming to her.

Chapter 2
The Great Fair

Four years had passed since Sixte had left to become a miller.

Four years that Celeste had taken care of the farm with her parents.

Four years that she found solace at the waterfall, when she could no longer bear their incessant instructions.

Carry this! Cut that! And don't forget the sheep!

What they need is a servant, not a daughter.

What are you looking at?

GO AWAY!

23

There, beneath the cool waterfall, she could forget everything.

It was as if the water washed away all of her anger and frustration...

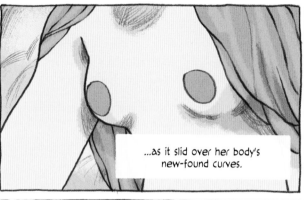

...as it slid over her body's new-found curves.

?!

But this morning, for the very first time...

What the...?

...the waterfall brought its share of questions and worries.

Where were you all afternoon? We needed you to bring the animals back in, and we couldn't find you anywhere.

I went down to the forest.

In the middle of preparing for the annual transhumance? You only think of yourself, don't you?

Celeste wanted to tell them about the pain in her stomach.

Is something wrong?

But her fears had slowly become tainted by a strange kind of shame.

No, I'm fine. Just a little tired.

I'll be fine...

24

Life resumed its slow, unchanging course.

Each night, Polyphemus, the terrible cyclops, would lock away his flock.

Among them, there was one lamb who was unlike any other.

Independent and rebellious, her only wish was to escape!

Aaah, if only....

...she could fly away!

Bravo! Excellent! Rarely have I seen such talent in an actress!

?!

St... stay back!

Calm down! I wish you no harm!

And honestly, I don't see what a big girl like you could possibly fear from a little man like me.

A simple flick from your finger would send me flying back into the valley.

You come from the valley?

25

I come and go as I please. In this valley and in all the others.

I am Nando, the peddler. The winding road is my life, and I know no border.

What do you peddle?

HA HA!

Whatever you need, even if you don't know it yet!

Spices and silks from faraway lands. Seeds of the sun and pieces of the moon. News of the world and imaginary rumors.

I've never seen so many rare things in one place!

And that which is rare is also precious!

What is the valley like?

Well... I'd say the contents of my baggage pale in comparison.

REALLY? And are there people like me there, too?

Hmm... To be honest, that's rather uncommon.

Although...

Although what?

It so happens, by a stroke of luck that might not be luck at all...

...I am on my way, at this very moment, to the Great Fair of Fallas...

...famous for the couple of giants who live there.

A couple? You mean a man and a woman?

Yes, that kind of couple.

That's incredible!

Why don't you accompany me there? You could meet them.

Oooh no! My parents wouldn't want me to go!

Your parents? Are they even bigger than you?

Not at all! Although my father's anger can be, sometimes.

Having said that, if he doesn't know about it... there's no risk of him getting angry.

What do you mean?

The valley of Fallas is only a few hours' march from here. With your stride, we could be back here before nightfall.

Are you sure about that?

Trust me, the mountain paths hold no secrets from Nando!

Let's go, then!

Guided by Nando, Celeste rushed down the hills she had longingly gazed at so often.

A new world seemed to spring up around her with every step.

And an exhilarating feeling began to well up inside her.

For the first time, she felt free and weightless.

Here we are!

The valley of Fallas and its annual Grand Fair!

The little houses! And the little farms! They're all so cute!

There must be lots of people inside them!

How I'd love to see them up close...

Well, what's stopping you?

It wouldn't be very prudent...

Barging into town in the middle of the fair wouldn't be prudent...

...but hiding inside the storehouse while the streets are empty shouldn't cause any trouble.

The storehouse?

It's the wooden building over there that looks out over the market. It will give you a perfect view of the city folk.

Incidentally, that's where the two giants are.

Away we go!

Are you sure I'll fit inside the building?

Hurry up, the coast is clear!

And as for fitting in there, if the other two can...

...you should have no trouble.

The storehouse of Fallas!

These are your giants?

Statues made of straw and paper...

I don't recall saying they were made of flesh and bone...

And that doesn't prevent the people in the valley from worshiping them.

Imagine how happy they would be if they met a living giant!

What are you talking about?

All you would have to do is put on the woman's outfit. You would look very convincing.

And you could get as close to the villagers as you pleased.

I... I don't know...

Trust me! This is going to be a magical moment.

And afterwards, you can go back home.

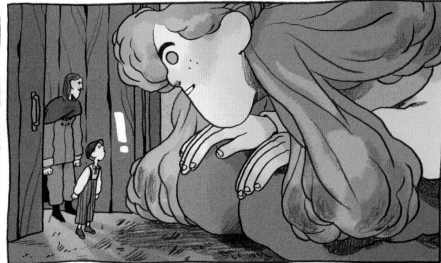

31

I didn't mean to scare him!

But that's what makes this so promising!

What's the point if they all run away the second I open my mouth?!

I may have a way to reassure them, but you must obey my instructions to the letter!

Obey you? Why not put a leash on me, while you're at it?

Calm down, it's just for show!

...but a leash is an excellent idea!

Thus began an endless procession of villagers.

Though uneasy at first, they were soon reassured by the peddler's apparent control over the giant.

Celeste agreed to humor their every request.

Wow!

From the most amusing...

HA HA HA

To the most absurd.

The afternoon and evening went by quickly before Celeste even realized it.

After nightfall, the requests became increasingly strange and insistent.

And just what does the creature eat? Rocks?

Exactly! Even though she prefers fresh meat!

That's nonsense!

Just chew on this and let me talk!

What about drinks? With a gullet like hers, she must be able to pound them down!

Quite right, friend! To her, a keg is nothing more...

...than a mere thimble!

Go on! It's just grape juice.

GLUB GLUB

IT'S TOO STRONG!

ARGH!

HA HA! FALLAS WINE IS THE BEST THERE IS!

BRING OUT ANOTHER KEG! I THINK SHE LIKES IT!

HA HA   HA   HA   HA !

I... I don't feel so good, Nando...

Come on, just a little more effort... it's almost over.

That creature of yours looks like a female to me! And well-built, too.

How much to let us have a look at her bosom?

100 pennies to peek at a breast! 500 to see it all!

NANDO! NO!

Come now, you can't say no to your audience.

THAT'S ENOUGH!

Wretched husbands! Drunkards, all of you!

She isn't here to be ogled by indecent eyes such as yours!

This is the daughter of the Giants of the Harvest! Don't forget our traditions!

Like them, she must follow the procession to the town square!

They're right! The hour of the Giants has come! It's time for the parade!

What's happening? We're leaving?

Something like that. You're going to get to visit the village, just like you wanted.

Even the best things come to an end.

This way.

Nando!

I'll catch up!

Everything began to spin around Celeste.

Shouts, laughter, and songs all merged together in a whirlwind of sound.

But upon reaching the town square, they were suddenly quiet, swallowed up by an ominous silence.

The time had come for the Giants to die...

...and for the villagers' fields to rise from their ashes.

NO! NOOO!

Terrified and overcome with sadness, Celeste watched the villagers flee in every direction.

I... I didn't want... this...

How could she ever have thought they would accept her?

She had but one desire.

To run away as far as she could...

...and to disappear into the night.

Chapter 3
The White Knight

When she awoke, the first thing that struck Celeste was the blinding light.

The second thing was the unpleasant smell of vomit.

What...? Where am I?

And the third thing was an infernal racket caused by some rather strange creatures.

Ah! She is starting to move again!

Hiiiiii!!

KLING KLANG

Make way! Make way!

Hail, noble country dwellers. Would you be willing to lend a hand to the arm of justice?

?

Who's that?

The Bailiff of Blasz and his White Knight of Parangon.

He seems to be in quite a mood this morning...

We are in search of a terrifying monster that devastated the Fallas town square last night.

Witnesses claim the creature is a foul mixture of ravenous ogre and ancient titan.

Good grief, he's raving about those monsters in his books again...

I thought the Bailiff had forbidden him to read them.

Your, uh, Trite Hen is over there.

So close? It is time to act!

Prepare yourself, knave! I am eager to give you a taste of Alba, my flashing blade!

Parangon... For pity's sake, don't get overexcited...

The trail is still fresh!

No doubt we are dealing with some stupid cyclops or other vile Hecatoncheire.

A Hecato what?

Books teach you strange things.

It's a hundred-armed monster, everyone knows that!

Aha! I now approach your putrid lair!

Show me your hideous face, if you dare...

Uh... good day...

S... same to you...

What a tall young woman...

You haven't seen a monstrous-looking creature, have you?

I... I don't think so, no...

Gadzooks! And yet, the tracks are unmistakable. Could he possess the power of invisibility?

But if you are seeking the one responsible for the damage done at Fallas last night, I'm afraid it's me.

But... beugh...! A damsel could never be a monster...

She can be innocent. Or in distress... at worst ...

And yet, I'm to blame...

But... beugh... th-that can't be... beugh, beugh!

What's with him?

He's beughing.

Perfect! A fault confessed is a fault half-punished!

Take her to the castle, Knight.

Take her... beugh! Of course...

I will refer her case to the Archbishop. After all, it's his job to deal with problems of this scale.

What about the swindler who was with her?

Not only did he bring her to the Fair, but he also took advantage of the confusion to rob the villagers of their earnings!

Then we shall put a price on his head. Let's say 500 coins for his capture. Dead or alive.

Oh no! You can't!

Enough! Knight, escort her to the dungeon.

And take care of the parchment-work.

A damsel in a dungeon?

Beugh!

Beneath the knight's helm, his thoughts chased each other back and forth incessantly.

No creature he had read about looked like Celeste.

While he was indeed conscious of the perils she was capable of unleashing...

...he could also sense that she was but a lost young girl.

For Celeste, things weren't much clearer.

She could not stop thinking about her parents.

Indeed, the mere thought of them discovering the catastrophe in Fallas overwhelmed her with shame.

She didn't know what scared her more.

That they thought she had run away...

...or that they had gone looking for her.

Here we are! The Chateau of the Blasz family!

Is this where you're going to lock me up?

Well, uh... if you don't offer any resistance, I could allow you to stay in the courtyard.

You won't even know I'm here... I promise.

"In each of his choices, in service to justice must the knight strive to remain."

How funny! Those sound like the words of Yvolf, in The Knight of the Wolf.

You know the book of Christian de Thebes?

One can live in the country and still have some education.

He's my favorite author! Gauthon the Dark One! Leandril the Welshman! Tristesir and Ysolde! What epic tales!

I don't know them all by heart...

You absolutely have to read them all!

Are you sure that won't be any trouble?

Not at all!

And that is how Paragon came to forget the giant and to only see the damsel...

...and how Celeste came to discover the man beneath the knight's armor.

44

Two weeks passed without the slightest word from the Bailiff or the Archbishop.

Convinced of Celeste's good faith, the knight agreed to let her come with him on his patrols.

During these long walks that they shared, they were able to discuss their favorite books at length...

In your opinion, which is more dangerous? The ogre or the cyclops?

In my opinion, it's all a question of point of view.

HA HA!

Excellent answer!

...and often ended up reenacting the famous adventures found within.

Look out! The giants!

Even so, Celeste never forgot about her family.

Sir Knight, I must confess something to you...

By all means, speak freely. As Megarne did to Ulrich...

...and I fear that they must be worried sick.

My parents who live in the mountains, have had no word from me for several weeks...

Without a doubt, delicate Celeste, your heart is most noble.

We have a pigeon loft. I will see to it your parents receive immediate word.

That would be wonderful.

But could you perhaps avoid mentioning the incident at Fallas?

Lying!

Beugh!

I cannot bring myself to do it!

I'm not denying my faults, Knight.

I'd just prefer hiding some of them until the Bailiff's verdict has been pronounced, that's all.

Hmmm... in that case, why not...

The young giantess was deeply touched by this act of trust.

Sleep well, generous Knight!

Y... you too, wise Celeste.

Beugh!

"White and immaculate..."

"...such was the handkerchief that Lady Genalva came to offer to Perciflor, her faithful knight."

"And such was the love they shared."

Gadzooks! That passage moves me to tears every time I read it!

It certainly is lovely. Even after the fifteenth reading...

But what if we set aside reading for something a little more exciting?

W... what?

46

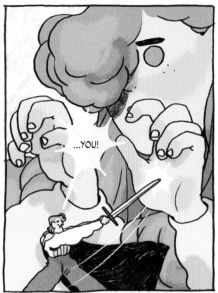

RAS!!

By the Old Mage's Beard! I'll treat your wounds! I'll just prepare a bandage...

Hey, enough already! Quit treating me like some kind of fragile decoration! I'm a tough, larger than life woman!

And put down those books of yours from time to time! Open your eyes!

And act!

Muoa.

I... I...

Beugh!

That night, the White Knight of Parangon did not return to the castle.

Celeste went to bed alone, still troubled by the afternoon's events.

Sweet Celeste! You were right!

For far too long, I have shirked my duty within stories and dreams.

But your beauty and words have opened my eyes.

Celeste...

Will you become my Lady?

But...? What...? Why?

Because our love is obvious.

But Parangon... are you really serious?

Of course! Just imagine: while I am out on a quest, you can decorate the castle to your liking, and pick out the next book for us to read together.

But... it was just a kiss.

I... I don't want to marry you...

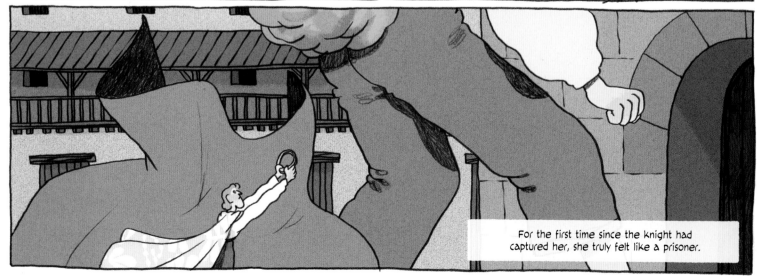

For the first time since the knight had captured her, she truly felt like a prisoner.

50

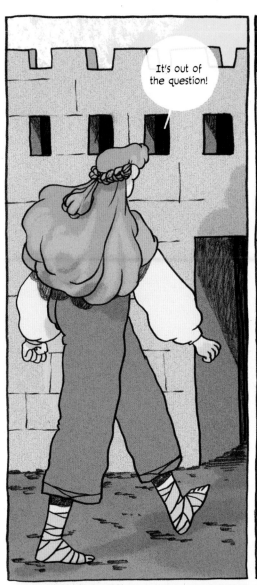

Chapter 4
Quarte the Warmonger

The time had come
to go back home.

Celeste had seen quite enough
of the valley and its men.

In order to avoid any
future encounters with the
Archbishop's men, she opted
to travel discreetly.

FRUS

She forged ahead in the
silence of the night...

Hiding by day in the hollows of steep ravines...

...or in the depths of dense forests.

ZZZZZZ

Soon, the mountain foothills
began to appear.

Nothing, however, could have prepared her for the new obstacles that were to soon stand in her way.

TAC TAC
TAC TAC

LA GUERRE EST DÉCLARÉE !!!

N ORDER TO REPEL THE INVASION OF THE ARCHBISHOPRIC BY THE DRAGONS OF THE DUCHY OF ALICASTRE, ALL ABLE-BODIED MEN ARE HEREBY CALLED TO THE MILITARY CHESSBOARD

Hail, young cowherds! What are you doing here?

Well... we're looking after our grazing cows.

This area is forbidden to civilians. You must go back down to the valley.

Oh? If you say so...

But there's no grass for our cows in the valley.

But you'll be safe from Alicastre's Dragons there!

We have received orders to evacuate the highland pastures...

...and to keep the inhabitants from being taken prisoner.

Ah, of course.

The folk from the Duchy of Alicastre have always been our neighbors. Some are even close cousins. They will not harm us.

I doubt the peasants who were taken prisoner after seeing their farms pillaged and burned would share your opinion.

Perhaps you approve of your cousins' schemes? Perhaps you may even know where we might find them?

Even if I did, I wouldn't tell you.

Let's be on our way, shall we?

Halt, boy! You're staying with us. I'm declaring you a Pawn of the Chessboard.

What? But...?

And bring a cow along with you. Each new recruit must pay tribute to the war effort.

You truly are despic...

CRACK!

The tables had suddenly turned.

BLAM!!

From now on, it was war.

Quick! Run!

What the...?

In a single second, all of her former woes seemed suddenly unimportant to her.

Her parents were in grave danger. She needed to find them as quickly as possible.

But this would be no easy task.

The valley's population was now cloistered away in their villages...

...and the Chessboard's troops regulated access to the mountain.

Adding to these difficulties were the rocky foothills, which deprived Celeste of her usual hiding places.

However, she found a solution...

...and was able to begin her ascent.

Stop, you're going to make me...

AAAH

Huh?

TSU!

Uh... who goes there?

Show yourself, sneezing foe!?

FRUS

FRUS

FRUS

HA HA HA HA HA HA HA!

Stop that! You're tickling me!

Celeste!

Quarte!

A woman!

I don't believe it!

What are you doing here? You're in the middle of a war zone!

Get back, Pawn Quarte! This is clearly an agent of the enemy!

Such a she-monster could only be on their side!

Impossible! I can vouch for her, Knight Bacchantes.

She's my little sister!

"Little" sister?

Can't wait to see the big one, then...

Heh heh!

We also have a father and a mother in the highland pastures whom I long to see.

No one is going up there! Our mission is to patrol the mid-mountain regions. Not to attack the enemy positions.

Hiiiii!!

The Dragons are already up there?

The Duchy has taken the far slopes and holds some of the high mountain passes.

They want to annex the entire mountain.

AND YOU'RE JUST SITTING HERE? WHILE OUR PARENTS ARE IN DANGER?!

I can't just do whatever I want! And you, what are you doing so far away from the farm?

Dragon-Eye! Are any of the Chessboard's pieces in sight?

Of course not! They are far too afraid to venture up here.

Unless...

What is it?

No... nothing... I thought I saw something moving in the trees...

It's okay, they didn't see us.

Let's make sure they close their eyes for good. Your move, Pawn Grosso.

Right away, sir!

What? You're not going to kill them, are you?

This is war, Celeste.

WAR IS A POOR EXCUSE!

SOUND THE ALARM! THE PAWNS ARE ATTACKING!

TO AAAARMS!

Oh, bravo, Celeste! Nice job!

We don't kill people!

We no longer have a choice, anyway!

FORWARD, PAWNS!

Release the boulders! They'll clear off the slope but good!

BROLOOM!!

Uh... T... t-take cover!

Wha...?

BROOM!

Ouch! Say, they don't kid around up there!

Because-we're-at-war!

What is that thing?

Did they change their Rook?

I doubt it's fireproof.

War... war... you really haven't changed a bit.

You're still the mean little boy who was always looking for a fight.

Put me down!

He was mean?

And grumpy, too!

THAT'S ENOUGH!

FLAAM!

61

BLAM!

BOO!

Noooooo!

We won!

Did you see that, Quarte? I'm not the worst fire-dung player there is!

The road to the highland pastures was now open. However, the Dragons' acts of oppression did not bode well.

The farm!

FUOOOOOOO

No home had been spared, it seemed.

64

Quarte, this can't be!

Curse them! We're going to make them pay!

They must have been so scared... I never should have left...

You got that right!

But I hope you had fun!

SIXTE! You're alive!

So are you, apparently!

And our parents?

Hiding in the old cave, higher up.

Out of stupidity or laziness, the Dragons didn't bother climbing up there.

My little one! I thought I'd never see you again!

I'm so sorry! I should have been here with you!

On the contrary! Who knows what those barbarians would have done if they found you!

You were right, my daughter! The mountain isn't the safest refuge...

We're to blame, too! We never should have tried to keep you here the way we did.

Mother! Father! I love you so much!

The time had now come to return to the safety of the valley.

Along the way, many lost peasants joined their group.

The taking of the pass had paved the way for a decisive counter-offensive, for which the Knight Bacchantes received the highest praise.

Celeste and her family would soon be able to return to their highland pastures.

Make way! Step aside!

Young red-haired girl of great size, dressed in rags, and answering to the name of Celeste.

Sounds like me...

Then please follow me: Monseigneur Porphyrus has ordered your arrest.

Who's that?

A Seraph. One of the Archbishop's elite soldiers.

On what charges? My sister has valiantly fought in your name.

She must appear before the Court of Davignan for pretending to be a monster, disturbing the peace, destroying the bell tower, and escaping from the Chateau of Blasz.

What?

He speaks true! I'm sorry, but it's high time I took responsibility for the mistakes I've made.

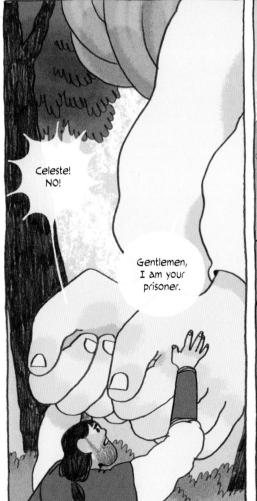

Celeste! NO!

Gentlemen, I am your prisoner.

Do you know of this Porphyrus, Quarte?

Why are you so afraid of him?

He is the High Inquisitor of Davignan.

And the worst of them all.

Chapter 5
The Inquisitor

The imminent arrival of a giant in Davignan did not fail to kindle people's interest.

Soon, they began to gather and jostle each other along the roads and paths, hoping for a chance to catch a glimpse of her.

Some were curious, even hostile.

But most were content to simply watch her as she walked by.

O Lord Porphyrus! May we beseech you to grant us a few moments of your precious time?

Come on! Move!

But I'll never be able to fit in there!

Sure you will!

AAAH!

That wasn't necessary.

Yeah, but it was fun.

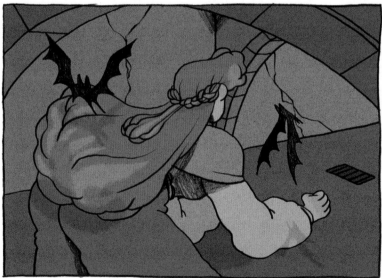

Are you okay, sweetheart? That swine didn't hurt you too much, did he?

Arvet is the worst guard of them all.

Is this the dungeon they reserve for women?

Not hardly... it seems that our femininity is our greatest crime in the eyes of Porphyrus.

What...? But why?

Because we're different, sweetheart! And that frightens him...

I would sell my charms for money. For Porphyrus, only the devil himself is worse...

Virgins don't fare much better.

The noble who employed Leonore got her pregnant.

He did not hesitate to get rid of her by accusing her of theft.

What about you?

Ohh, I just had the foolish audacity to become an actress.

Nina is a woman who changes roles. That's almost worse than being a harlot!

What you say is true.

But the one Porphyrus hates more than any other is the Witch.

The Witch?

A woman who possesses infinite knowledge, capable of altering both life and death.

There's no such thing as the Witch! She's just a legend to amuse children!

She does, too, exist, young lady!

But even if she didn't, the mere possibility would be enough to drive him mad with rage.

And you, what are you in here for?

I destroyed a bell tower and hurt several people.

For once, someone is in here for actually committing a crime...

Come, we'll make some room for you.

72

This way, giantess!

The Inquisitor wants to see you.

Usually, he prefers conducting interrogations in the lower dungeons...

But sometimes, one must adapt.

Place your hands through these.

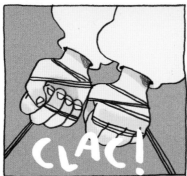

CLAC!

CLAC!
CLAC!
CLAC!

The prisoner is ready, Inquisitor. As you requested.

Where is she?

Wh... who?

You know very well who I'm talking about...

The Witch? I don't know her.

73

LIAR!

You're just like all the other females of your kind.

Treachery sticks to your very flesh.

But I know how to make you admit the truth.

Arvet!

CLAC!
CLAC!

Did the Witch create you?

My parents found me in the mountains...

Nonsense! Tell me where she is hiding!

CLAC!
CLAC!
CLAC!

I know nothing about her!

Perhaps she doesn't even exist!

Of course she does! She dwells within each and every one of you!

In your gazes, your smiles, your sinful curves ...

And I intend to deliver us all from them!

Despite her apparent show of bravado, Celeste was unable to sleep that night.

She was unable to understand the Inquisitor's narrow-mindedness.

And yet, she still refused to give up hope.

Psssst...Over here...

White Knight! What are you doing here?

I've come to free you, Lady Celeste!

I shall knock out the guards, steal their keys, and we shall flee into the night.

And then what will we do?

D... don't get me wrong! I haven't forgotten your request.

No tie binds you to me, if you do not wish it...

Your offer is most noble, Sir Knight. But I must decline.

But why? You are clearly innocent.

And it is for that very reason that I wish to explain myself in public, in front of everyone.

Gadzooks, Lady Celeste! I am humbled, once again, by your magnanimity.

In Davignan, justice was served by the Confessional Tribunal.

The Father-Prosecutor presented the crimes of the accused, who then had to explain himself before the Tribunal and the assembly.

It was the Inquisitor, however, who was responsible for pronouncing the sentence of the Almighty.

The crowd hungered for these public confessions...

...although everyone present that day hoped the sentence would not be too harsh.

Defendant Celeste, can you tell us by what devious means you arrived in Fallas?

It wasn't premeditated... I mean... I just wanted to see the valley.

So it was curiosity, then! A most vile sin indeed. And a typically female one.

I should never have gone there. I sincerely regret it.

Just as you regret disguising yourself as a monster in order to frighten the villagers.

Witnesses I and II.

Yes, it's true! She scared my little Leander.

I was real, real, real scared.

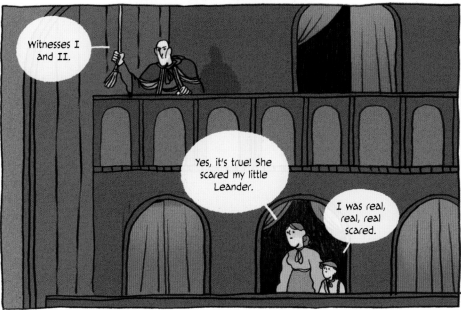

Why isn't she talking about that damned peddler?

I imagine she wants to cover for him... or maybe she feels responsible for everything.

I did that, too. I admit it. It was a mistake.

A "mistake"? Your discernment appears to be rather limited!

How would you describe the rest of the evening? Was it spent frivolously?

Witnesses III and IV.

She was drinking! Drinking, I tell you!

And then she tried to tempt us!

NO!

Well, yes I did...

But it wasn't my fault.

And the destruction of the bell tower? That wasn't your fault, either?

And neither were the consequences upon these peaceful villagers?

Witnesses V and VI!

It all came crumbling down! It was like the Apocalypse!

A shingle almost crushed my foot!

I... I'm sincerely sorry... truly...

SILENCE, DEFENDANT!

The proof of your guilt is clear!

But the worst has yet to come! Tell us of your ties to the Witch!

Her again! I've never even seen the Witch!

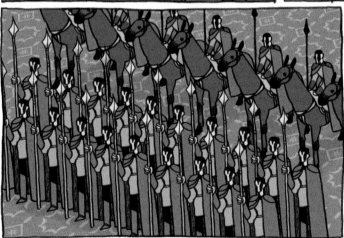

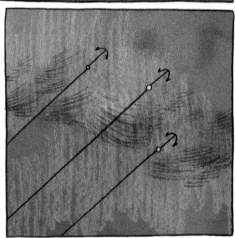

BY ALBA! Lady Celeste, I ride to your aid!

Parangon!

Take care of that buffoon. And ready the lightning!

Parangon the White to the bitter end shall fight...

FSSSSS

BOOM!

Celeste could not say whether the pain came from the impact...

...or from having to concede defeat.

OUCH!

My shoulder!

Pain is the first step towards redemption.

Tomorrow, the stake shall wipe away all your sins.

And in case you were thinking of escaping...

...know that I am holding your parents hostage.

Comply, and they shall be freed. Refuse, and they will follow you to Hell.

Y... you're a monster!

Three of your fellow cellmates shall accompany you into the flames.

They shall certainly share your point of view.

PORPHYRUS!

What did I ever do to you?

You exist.

83

You really exist?

Looks that way...

And my parents?

They are safe. I helped them escape.

Your powers are incredible.

Does sabotaging a dam truly seem so amazing to you?

Now come, follow me.

The time has come for us to disappear.

Chapter 6
The Witch

How long did their journey last? Celeste could not say.

For hours, days, entire nights perhaps, they glided down the river.

Little by little, they plunged into a world made of water, mist, and silence.

The world of the Marsh.

We have arrived! You will be safe here.

I don't know how to thank you! Know that I shall always be your devoted servant.

Arise, young woman. I didn't save you to take your freedom away.

But she's right, Witch. Without you, we would now be nothing but ashes.

That accursed Porphyrus needed to be reminded that women are not kindling.

And call me Laelith. The title of Witch only has meaning to the Inquisition.

But you do have powers?

The only magic I possess is knowledge and learning.

Two domains that still possess an aura of mystery.

A temple?

For generations, we have taken turns trying to pierce the secrets of these marshes.

And some of them may very well concern you, Celeste.

This is incredible... It's as though this place was built for people my size.

I think that may be the case.

Despite appearances, the world has not always known today's unyielding order.

In ancient times, when we still lived among the caves and rocks, it is more than likely that women ruled.

In those long-gone days, kings were queens, and gods were goddesses.

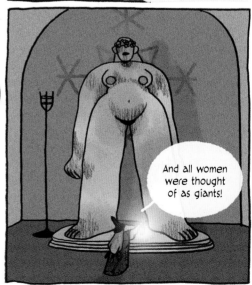

And all women were thought of as giants!

She looks just like you...

It's troubling...

Then, the centuries passed. Men trained animals and tamed the earth.

They alone appeared to possess the miraculous power of giving life.

And they discovered the role that their own seed played.

The power of creation was now a shared one.

Their strength and pride did the rest.

And then you came. You, a reminder of that long-lost era.

Do really think there's a connection?

I don't know, Celeste. But I would be happy to help you find out.

It would be an honor!

The offer is extended to you all!

I will teach you all I know, and together we will unlock the secrets of nature and the marshes.

Stay here as long as you like. And never forget that you are free to leave whenever you wish.

Even though Celeste and her friends hardly regretted their decision, the discovery of the island where Laelith lived brushed away any doubts they might have had.

Its roots burrow deep into the very heart of reality.

There, it draws upon the numbers, letters, and arts that make up its trunk.

Knowledge is like a giant tree!

Then it expands into branches and ramifications that are brimming with knowledge.

And finally, it ends in the shimmering foliage of books, which you must read in order to understand every last line.

Once again, the time soon came to say goodbye.

Celeste, my darling little one...

I have nothing to fear here, Mother. And so much to learn!

The farm will always be your home!

Never forget that, my daughter!

Celeste, Nina, Leonora, and Mariam soon discovered a new way to spend their days, one completely dedicated to studying and discussion.

And yet, reading made up but a small part of their day.

Theory is only necessary if it anticipates and perpetuates itself through practice.

VLAM!!

Studying plants...

Dissecting animals...

Observing the rotation of dancing stars in the sky...

Celeste's thoughts wavered between the infinitesimal and the infinite.

Regularly, Laelith would leave the Marsh to meet with wisdom-seekers.

Under no circumstances should our knowledge remain unshared.

Our understanding of the world must spread, in order to help those in need.

Potions, remedies, ointments... I will reveal their ingredients and uses to you.

Barely a month after their arrival, Celeste was given a chance to deepen her knowledge of the secrets of creation.

RAAAH!

My stomach! It emptied all of a sudden!

Don't worry! Your waters just broke. It's perfectly normal.

TAP TAP TAP

Your child shall be here soon. We must get ready to welcome it and help it find its way.

It was thus that Celeste discovered the beauty of creation...

I... I want to walk...

Then walk!

...and its extraordinary power.

Bring the bathtub, Celeste!

RAAAH!

For the first time, she witnessed this miracle, so often repeated...

...and yet always unique.

THAT WAS UNBELIEVABLE! SO MOVING!

He's so small, yet so strong.

It almost makes you want one of your own, eh?

Uh... yes... perhaps.

Believe me, there's no rush.

It's better to savor what happens nine months before that. It's a far more enjoyable experience.

Enjoyable...?

You... you've never been with a man?

SURE I HAVE!

Well, I kissed one, once...

And what did you think of it?

It too often is.

Well... it was wet and fast.

And by yourself, you've never...

Do you see?

What, by myself?

Gracious, what a shame!

What we're trying to tell you, is that you don't need a man to give yourself pleasure.

And you're allowed to have pleasure without it bringing a baby into the world.

But... you think that will work for me, too?

I assure you: all women ask themselves that question.

Just give it a try! You have nothing to lose!

Celeste was deeply troubled by this discussion.

But far less than the wave of warmth that washed over her a few nights later.

OH OH OH OH YESSSS!

A certain routine soon set in. But this caused no feelings of exhaustion for Celeste.

She spent her days studying the giants' rune-writings...

BRAOUM!

It's Porphyrus and his men. They persist, they intrude, they push forward, ever deeper.

But the Marsh will always drive them back.

As water has always driven back fire.

CLAC!

94

Later that same month, Celeste and Nina had a strange encounter at the edge of the Marsh.

RAAAAAH! BY PLAUTUS! WOE IS US!

THIS DAMNED WAGON WILL NEVER MOVE AGAIN!

Stuck in the muck like a duck out of luck.

Scarpon! Moon! Is it really you?

A Princess? A ballerina? Could this be our lovely Nina?

What are you doing here?

The tour was a disaster...

Now here we are, all bogged down!

My friend Celeste can help you!

That's real nice, Nina, but I highly doubt she can...

...do anything...

Are you traveling salesmen?

The only thing we sell is the fruit of our passion!

We are actors.

We belonged to the same troupe until Porphyrus had me arrested.

That sure was a close call...

Follow me! I'll show you where we live.

Are you sure, Nina?

Of course! They'll only be staying a night or two.

And it was thus that Scarpon and Moon brought a little piece of the outside world into the very heart of the Marsh.

The news of the world was good.

Porphyrus' authority was increasingly challenged.

And his inability to capture the Witch had caused him to lose favor in high places.

As for the two actors' other anecdotes, Celeste preferred not to listen to them.

Nothing in the world could make her think that there could be a place where life was more perfect than in the Marsh.

However, the next day, when Nina expressed her desire to leave, Celeste reacted strongly.

BUT YOU KNOW VERY WELL HOW BRUTAL AND TREACHEROUS THE OUTSIDE WORLD IS!

HEY! I'll be fine! I'm a big girl, too.

But we have everything we need here! And we're happy together!

Nina isn't doing this to hurt you, Celeste. She is free to go.

I... I want to join them, too.

Listen to what your heart tells you, Leonora. That is our motto!

However, while leafing through the pages of a Persian treatise on medicine, they made an important discovery.

The giants' highborn bloodline seemed to have disappeared within the space of a few short decades.

To help Celeste overcome this separation, Laelith quickly encouraged her to resume their research of the giants of old.

But the rare volumes on the subject mainly described the males, and often in rather unflattering terms.

Which tended to suggest that they had either been victims of a swift epidemic...

...or of a sickness that prevented them from reproducing.

These... these are only hypotheses, Celeste...

It would be so sad...

CELESTE! MARIAM! I NEED YOU!

What's happening? Is she ill?

She's pregnant. And she took the wrong herbs to flush out the child.

Flush it out?

Not all pregnancies are desired. It must be removed.

Mariam, go fetch the potions and my instruments.

Celeste, go boil some water.

But... we can't kill a child?!

NOW IS NOT THE TIME, CELESTE! THIS WOMAN IS IN GRAVE DANGER!

Either help us, or get out of our way.

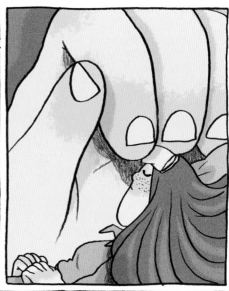

It is done. The potion has taken effect.

It's over!

She made it. Thanks to you two.

Laelith, how can you do that?

The question you should be asking is, "Why must I do it?"

It is not my role to agree with or contest it. I am not a judge but a healer.

And I must accept that others' freedom is vital.

Do you understand?

Yes, I think so.

Another season came and went. Little by little, Celeste became aware of the vast cycle of life.

She allowed herself to be carried along by its ebb and flow, feeling its regular rhythm...

...and only raising her head to question the skies.

The following winter saw Porphyrus attempt yet another excursion into the Marsh.

Recently dismissed, he had hired a band of brigands and mercenaries.

But despite all of his hatred, he failed once more to make it through the twists and turns of the swamplands.

Weary, his men ended up abandoning him...

...leaving him to sink alone into the thick mud.

Porphyrus is no more.

His stubbornness led him to his downfall.

We're finally going to be able to live and study in peace.

I'm leaving, Celeste.

WHAT?

What do you mean?

Knowledge is acquired, accentuated, and passed on. It is time for me to pass the mantle on to another.

Mariam has told me of her wish to succeed me here.

You are free to do the same, Celeste.

Even though I sense that your place is elsewhere, in the vast world around us.

I... I don't understand...

The Marsh is a place of refuge and learning. Under no circumstances must it become a fortress where people lock themselves away.

You still have much to learn about yourself and what you want to do with your life.

One cannot live free while hiding...

100

For several long weeks, Celeste did nothing but walk, as if needing to rid herself of the stagnant immobility she had become accustomed to in the Marsh.

Calm had returned to the Archdiocese since Porphyrus's demise, and Celeste could now move about freely.

Many villagers had also heard tell of her work with Laelith and her countless good deeds in the area.

And yet, Celeste kept her distance from the villages, often approaching them only at sunrise or sunset.

Indeed, the giantess had an idea in mind, a longing that would allow her to link the past with the future.

It finally became a reality one spring evening, as Nina and her troupe were about to give a performance at the town square of a small village.

The Earth is a theater! The horizon is its stage!

And tonight, under cover of night, the troupe of the Vast World shall reveal its mysteries to you.

Allow yourselves to fall under the spell of Circea the Enchantress...

Reeeeeee

...and her zealous servants.

Scarpon! Moon! Come look at what has just appeared at the bottom of my cauldron!

It looks like a stage, within a village...

By the gods, it's incredible!

...where little by little appear unlikely visages.

Is it dream or reality?

Who can say? What is real? What is fake?

Who is dreaming? Who is awake?

AAAH

ha ha ha ha ha ha ha ha ha ha

Before the dazzled eyes of Celeste and the crowd gathered before her, a marvelous spectacle had just begun.

In an incessant whirlwind, fantastic creatures appeared...

Sirena, the singer of the oceans!

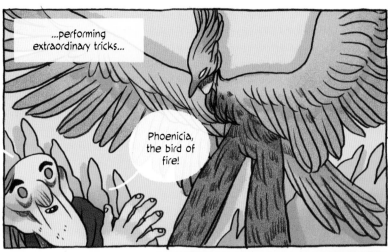

...performing extraordinary tricks...

Phoenicia, the bird of fire!

Adam, the first juggler!

...before ever-changing backgrounds.

CLONC

Oops!

CLACK

CLONC

But the magical extravaganza reached its climax with the performance of Alto...

...the Strider of Skylines.

Defying wind, great heights, and vertigo, he has made pacing the sky his ultimate goal!

HOOOOO!!

No!

BRAVO!!

Celeste, sweetheart! I was so happy to see you in the crowd!

Your performance was marvelous! I loved it!

We owe all of these creations to Tirso!

Allow me to return the compliment, young Celeste!

Nina had told me all about her big friend, but my imagination did not do you justice.

Celeste? Now if that isn't a name to attract tightrope walkers.

Your act was positively dizzying.

You really had us scared!

You, at least, tried to catch me.

Not everyone would...

Some nights, I wonder what the crowd hopes for the most: for me to fall, or to catch myself.

You shouldn't say that...

Don't you mind him. Alto isn't exactly an optimist.

Those below hardly encouraged me to become one.

So rarely, in fact, that I swore never to touch the ground again.

Freedom only exists among the clouds.

You of all people ought to know that.

What are you going to do now?

Why don't you join our troupe? I foresee an... immense... potential!

I... I don't know...

My rare attempts at acting didn't exactly turn out well...

But maybe I could work backstage? Changing backgrounds or operating machinery?

That's a wonderful idea!

Oh, yes! I couldn't refuse such an opportunity!

But that doesn't mean you're exempt from coming up with your own act.

There is art inside each of us.

And you must find yours in order to truly become a member of the troupe of the Vast World.

The very next day, Tirso showed Celeste around backstage.

RAS

The giantess's size and intelligence immediately worked wonders.

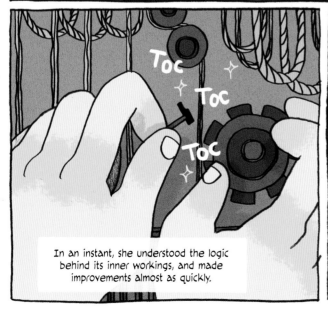

TOC TOC TOC

In an instant, she understood the logic behind its inner workings, and made improvements almost as quickly.

THE VAST WORLD

With Celeste in charge, the theater of the Vast World reached new heights.

108

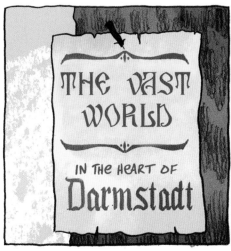

THE VAST
WORLD

IN THE HEART OF
Darmstadt

Quickly, their reputation grew and they soon found themselves invited to venues in faraway, prestigious locations.

Night after night, Celeste made sure the show ran smoothly...

...as she impatiently awaited Alto's act.

The young man's determination fascinated her...

...and placed him above all others, forevermore.

The joy of traveling and new discoveries did not turn Celeste's attention away from finding her very own act.

And although there was no shortage of inspiration...

Juggling planets!

A shell game with animals!

A Cyclopean hillside.

...the results always fell short of her lofty expectations.

All I do is use my size as a gimmick, without inventing anything new.

Think of your secrets, Celeste. And your desires. That's how you will find your act.

One morning, as she was enjoying the calm of the stage, she watched Alto as he practiced.

His high wire was stretched out in a long, steep diagonal...

...which he tried to scale with an unfamiliar look of rage on his face.

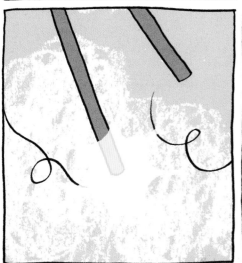

This time, I caught you!

Who asked you to?

What makes you think that I didn't want to go back to the ground for good?

Why are you so angry, Alto?

110

What else should I feel? Can't you see that life is nothing but violence and destruction?

Nina never told you what the people below did to my family and village?

The ground isn't worth a thing, Celeste.

I only feel good up there, with the weight of mankind lifted from my shoulders.

That's not the impression I got when I arrived...

In the weeks that followed, Alto isolated himself in silence.

Celeste felt lost.

Remember what Laelith used to say: "You cannot fight another man's demons for him."

Nina confirmed the tragic fate of Alto's family, and how Tirso had adopted him when he was only 5 years old.

Above all, Celeste realized that the Witch hadn't taught her about the oh-so-vivid pain caused by worry.

Whether direct consequence or pure coincidence, it was in the throes of this inner turmoil that Celeste found her act.

It suddenly seemed obvious to her.

As was her desire to devote it to Alto and to him alone.

Bravo, little one. You've found your act.

It's beautiful and true, just like what you told me the other day.

I'm sorry for your family, Alto.

My kin have always been scapegoats...

The truth is, I'm terrified...

The anger, the violence down below... I can feel them inside me!

And it drives me crazy!

Alto, there's nothing wrong with feeling emotions. Even if they are frightening.

Your family is surely resting in peace, somewhere high above...

But you need to try to live down here. And to learn how to recognize those who love you.

The weeks that followed were some of the happiest that Celeste had ever known.

The discovery of their mutual feelings...

Moua.

THE VAST WORLD

The ever-changing landscapes, the endless performances...

It all formed an exhilarating whirlwind from which they only escaped to find each other.

Of course, Alto wasn't immune to the occasional relapse.

But with patience, discussion, and laughter...

Alto?

...Celeste always managed to restore his faith in life down here.

In those moments suspended in time, the lovers of the Vast World felt invincible.

My friends, my friends!

His Serene Highness wants to see us perform.

He has invited us to come to Dorsodoro as soon as possible!

We are going to see the City of Water! This is incredible!

Is it pretty there?

Are you kidding? It's the city where dreams become reality!

What do you think of it, prince of the air?

As someone who has already seen it, I'd say it's not bad...

You just have to be careful not to chase the wrong dream...

115

Chapter 8
The City of Water

Far to the east, beyond the kingdom of Alicastre and the plains of the Holy Empire, there exists a city-state that is said to be suspended between the sky and the sea.

Dorsodoro the Serene.

At the crossroads of the West and East, she welcomes the riches, spices, and mysteries of the entire world to her lagoon.

And it was in the heart of her most famous concert hall, the Theater of Pearl, that Celeste and her troupe were about to perform.

His Serene Highness! Prince Sandro Di Canoccia! He is here in person!

Of course he's here! He is the one who invited us!

It is of paramount importance not to disappoint him. The Theater of Pearl has decided the future of more than a few troupes.

Succeeding here is like triumphing before the whole world.

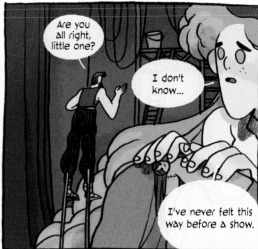

Are you all right, little one?

I don't know...

I've never felt this way before a show.

Are all those nobles in their fancy clothes bothering you?

Forget them, they're nothing!

How do you do it, Alto? It's like you're never worried?!

You need to quit caring about the spectators... I perform my act for the wind and skies.

For all that is beautiful and celestial...

Everything is going to be fine! You handle the marionette like a dream.

Take a deep breath for the first seconds, then follow her lead.

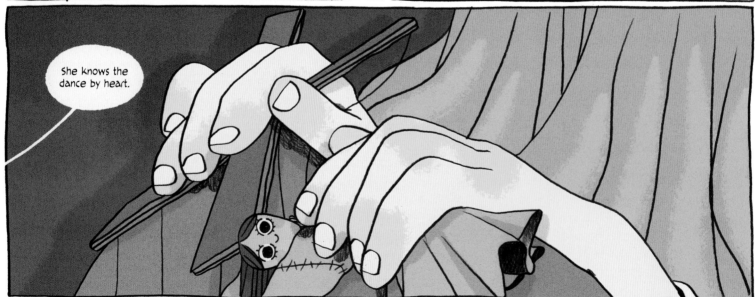

She knows the dance by heart.

Alto was right.

Once she overcame her stage fright, Celeste performed her act with extreme finesse.

The other acts followed, the backgrounds came and went...

...and silence fell at the end of the performance...

...before being shattered by the audience's applause.

Just listen to them! They loved it!

Perfect! You were all simply perfect!

Ahem.

Ahem.

TAP
TAP
TAP

His Serene Highness, the Prince Sandro Di Canoccia. And the Queen Mother Della Atriccia.

No, no... do not kneel! That isn't necessary.

I simply came to tell you that your performance delighted me.

You effortlessly weave dreams and reality together. You combine the intimate with the immense.

Many thanks, O Prince.

To be honest, I would like to make you an offer.

Are you quite certain, my Prince?

I would like to welcome you here and grant you financial support in order for you to create a new show.

Your choice of subject is, of course, completely up to you. My sole pleasure will be to have contributed to its creation.

And to see you perform it!

It is impossible to refuse such an honor, my Prince!

Perfect! I also wish to speak with the puppeteer Celeste.

Uh... yes, my Prince...

It is rare to meet an artist with talents such as yours, and I would like to invite you to my Palazzo, if you wish.

Of... of course.

Wonderful! Gondolino, my royal steward, will give you a golden fish: it opens all the doors to my palace.

It shall be done as you wish, Serene Highness.

It was built on a very particular rocky peak, which continuously grows.

This is fantastic!

Thus, the Palazzo overlooks the lagoon higher and higher each day.

And you, Celeste? Do you keep growing?

I try... In one way or another.

Anyway, thank you for coming to see me.

You didn't think I would?

You could have refused. Or felt that your place was not here.

As far as spaciousness goes, I don't think that will be a problem.

An ancient legend claims that our family descended from a line of giants.

Real... Really?

If you're interested, I would be happy to open the archives of our genealogists to you.

That would be both unexpected and undreamed-of!

Welcome to the aquatic library of the Palazzo.

Generation after generation, while the peak reaches upwards, we dig deeper into its depths in order to pour knowledge into it.

Wow!

Laelith would have loved it here... Your collection is positively gigantic!

And it is worth nothing if no one reads from it. That's why I had it opened to everyone who wishes to learn: men, women, or children.

You allow women to come here! That's dangerously progressive!

I know that for many, it seems unnatural.

But I was raised by a Queen, among sisters...

I could not see myself depriving them of anything.

What...? This looks like the skull of a...

A cyclops! All the evidence points towards it, anyway.

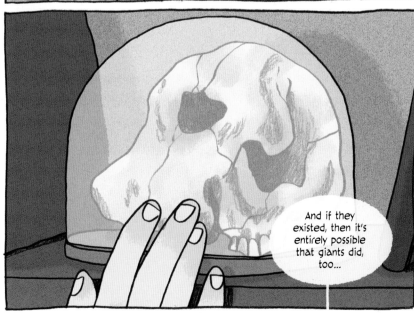

And if they existed, then it's entirely possible that giants did, too...

There is so much yet to learn and discover!

Come here as often as you like, Celeste.

Nothing would make me happier!

BLAM!!

So, this prince of yours? Not too charming?

He can't hold a candle to the king of the skies.

I suspected as much, to be honest.

But his library is incredible! He owns rare spell books! You have to see it!

You know how fond I am of parchment and old papers...

But go back, if you want to.

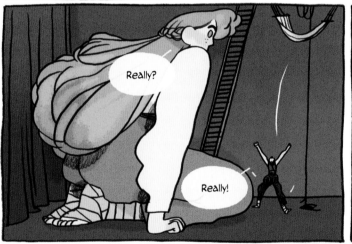

Really?

Really!

Celeste would often return to the Aquatic Library, losing herself in its endless bookshelves.

Thousand-year genealogy; unknown myths; comparative anatomy; each of her discoveries concerning giants gave her hope that they actually existed.

When the volumes were written in dorsodetto, the language of the lagoon, the Prince himself would provide translation.

The time they spent together seemed to rush by like a torrent, and it was not uncommon for them to find themselves alone, once the library's visitors had all left.

I haven't had a chance to tell you, Celeste, but your puppeteer act deeply moved me.

Your marionette's dance was incredibly tender and melancholy.

That was precisely my intention, my Prince.

One can feel your need to exist at our level.

But you must not regret your height.

It is what makes you so beautiful, so strong, and so unique.

Th... thank you, my Prince. That's very touching.

Above all, it's sincere.

Celeste! Celeste?

Are you with us?

I'm sorry, what?

For my new costume, I can't choose between old minstrel and toga-wearing poet.

Hold on, Tirso! Don't ask too much of her!

Pshh! You're talking nonsense...

A choice made today, by our lovely Celeste, could cause her misery as well as distress.

Truly? Between passion and reason, feelings and vision...

...Prince or aerialist, what's your decision?

125

You two are beginning to annoy me!

Yes, I spend a lot of time at the Palazzo! Yes, I enjoy Sandro's company!

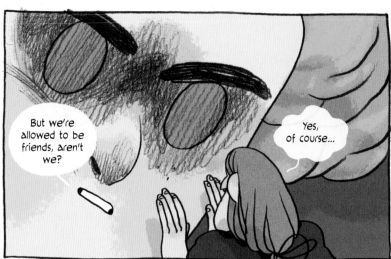

But we're allowed to be friends, aren't we?

Yes, of course...

And besides, honestly, talking to him isn't unpleasant at all.

It's a change from comedy duos, or solo acts like Alto's!

Well, you may not be honest, but at least you're blunt...

A... Alto! That's not what I meant to say...

Wait...

ALTO!

Though Celeste searched every street and canal in Dorsodoro, Alto, sadly, was nowhere to be found.

And when, chagrined, she stopped searching, she discovered that her steps had led her, once more, back to the Palazzo.

126

Forward, equinox jouster!

You'll fall in the water before I do, Amadeo!

It looks like your large friend has come to pay you a visit, Sandro.

She looks much more impressive on stage.

Ohh! No! Amadeo has beaten me yet again!

I... I'll be on my way. I didn't mean to intrude.

No, Celeste, stay! It's no problem at all.

We were just leaving, anyway.

We were?

Hush...

I'm sorry, I shouldn't have come.

On the contrary. I am glad you met my nieces and nephew.

I imagine you plan on having children with Alto?

Oh? Uh... I...

Excuse me, my question was too personal. It's none of my business.

To tell you the truth, I've never really brought up the subject.

Perhaps because I was afraid of his answer.

Once again, you don't have to say another word.

Come on! Since you're here, I'd like to show you a place that's very dear to my heart.

I used to come to this part of the lagoon often when I was younger. We call it "the Starry Mirror."

Certain legends say that a storm of falling stars crashed into its depths.

Others say that it's made of the scales of the Fish-World that fell here as it crossed the sky.

But in both legends, it is said that the mirror only shines for those who are still capable of amazement.

Do you know how to swim? At least you can touch the bottom.

But... you're crazy...

Don't tell me you're afraid! I was already doing this when I was only 7.

BLAOUF!

Wow! Now that's what I call making a splash!

The view of Dorsodoro from the water's surface was sumptuous.

Light and reflections sent the city reaching up to the sky and down into the depths of the water.

Oh, my Prince! The lagoon!

It's magnificent!

Everything seems so much more simple and pleasant when you are near.

You and I could experience such wonderful things together...

My Prince... I understand what you're feeling... but...

Say no more... I should not have told you that.

I do not wish to be the one to come between you and Alto.

Feel free to keep coming to visit me.

Or don't, if it makes you uncomfortable.

Celeste wandered for a long time that night, along the lagoon and the surrounding shores.

A thousand questions and a thousand desires flashed through her mind, where love, faithfulness, and freedom were all entwined.

At dawn, she decided to confide in the only person capable of helping her.

Are you kidding? You really went swimming with the Prince?!

Yes... well, it just happened.

Just stop it! I really don't know what to do!

And he didn't even try to kiss you? This is crazy!

He's so perfect! And adorable...

And at the same time, I can't just abandon Alto after all we've been through.

What would he do on his own...

Do you hear yourself?

What do you mean?

Are you afraid for Alto because he needs your help?

Or are you afraid for both of you, because you're still in love with him?

You're right. I'll go talk to him.

Chapter 9
The Queen Mother

The marriage of His Serene Highness, Prince Sandro Di Canoccia, to the giantess Celeste was celebrated on the first day of the month of equinoxes.

As far as the Dorsodorians could recall, it was the most sumptuous ceremony ever witnessed.

It was rumored that the Princess's wedding gown had required weeks of work, and had emptied several ponds of their pearl oysters.

The bride's train required no less than an entire family to carry.

As was customary, His Serene Highness was the first to cross the Bridge of Promises.

Celeste then joined him, cheered on by thunderous applause.

Together they exchanged vows, before the central pillar, where the protective statue of Hippocampo stood.

The jubilation was complete and the fish-lanterns lit up the lagoon all through the following night.

134

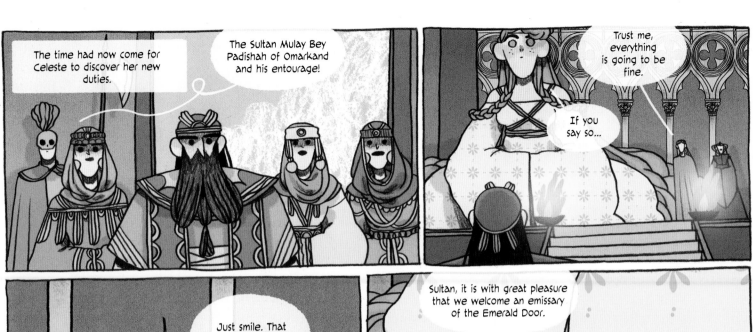

The time had now come for Celeste to discover her new duties.

The Sultan Mulay Bey Padishah of Omarkand and his entourage!

Trust me, everything is going to be fine.

If you say so...

Just smile. That should be enough.

Sultan, it is with great pleasure that we welcome an emissary of the Emerald Door.

But it pales in comparison to my pleasure in meeting your oh-so-famous wife.

Princess, you appear to possess extraordinary vigor.

As do your lovely daughters.

My daughters? What daughters?

Please excuse her, Mulay. She is not yet familiar with the traditions of Omarkand, and was unaware that these are your latest wives.

Ohhh, age is of little importance, you know. The only things that matter are the desire and devotion to serve one's husband.

Your words ring true and I hope the Princess shall learn from them.

She is a large woman. She must possess the wisdom of at least five wives.

Man, woman, child, it seems to me that all individuals deserve the same attention and the same consideration.

HA HA HA HA!

I recognize Dorsodoro's optimistic progressivism in your words.

Don't worry, I admire forwardness.

Especially in women...

THAT WAS INADMISSIBLE! WE BARELY AVOIDED AN INTERNATIONAL INCIDENT!

Imagine if he had been offended by your wife's words!

You exaggerate, Mother. You know very well how the Sultan enjoys engaging in self-caricature.

You must learn how to keep your wife in her place!

Learn how to keep your own, first! Whether you like it or not, Celeste is now Her Serene Highness of Dorsodoro.

Utter poppycock! She will only rightfully hold that title when you have impregnated her! Until then, she is nothing!

Enough, Mother! You go too far!

Let it be, my Prince.

The Queen Mother has made it most clear what she believes my role to be.

Even though I would never proclaim them so callously.

It may put her mind at ease knowing that it corresponds with my own desires.

Hold your wife in check, Sandro. She's out of line.

Neither Celeste nor the Prince could sleep that night.

Sandro did all he could to comfort her and assure her that her reaction was perfectly justified.

But the Queen Mother's words had cut into her like a painful stinger.

One she didn't know how to remove.

To avoid the Queen Mother, Celeste left the royal officiating to her.

Not one to remain inactive, she oversaw the inner workings of the Palazzo.

Quickly, servants, valets, cooks, and boatmen became her close friends.

She showed interest in each of them, asking about their families and their health.

Thus she won the hearts of all.

One day, a hairdresser told her of her sick son.

Celeste recognized the symptoms of an illness whose remedy she had learned from the Witch.

She had the ingredients brought to her, and she prepared it for the child.

138

After hearing about the potion's efficiency, many other servants came to see her.

Rumors began to spread and grow about how Her Serene Highness could heal all ailments.

People from all over the region flocked to the gates of the Palazzo.

The Prince supported Celeste in this endeavor by reopening an ancient chapel, located at the tip of the harbor, which had formerly been used as a place of quarantine.

Celeste came to spend more and more time there, taking care of all who needed her help for free.

The ancient Our Lady of the Mists church soon came to be known as Celeste's Chapel.

One spring morning, a ship with an unexpected captain landed nearby.

CELESTE!

Tertio?

So, Princess, how is life in the castle?

Ohhh, it's quite different than what you might think.

It's just like you to demean yourself while your popularity and generosity have already spread beyond the country's borders.

I'm just trying to make myself useful.

Let's talk about you instead. Where are you sailing from?

From faraway Omarkand, where it appears you have left a lasting mark on a certain soft-bellied Sultan.

Look at the present he had us bring here for your Prince.

It's a kind of tribute, according to him...

I'll see if I can find an animal to send back to him.

Their reunion was joyful but brief. Tertio only stayed long enough to unload and sell his cargo, and to purchase new goods.

And as his sails drifted farther and farther away, Celeste thought of the past, back when they lived on the mountain, and everything still seemed possible.

141

Autumn was misty in Dorsodoro, with a cold wind blowing in from the sea.

Eight months had passed, and the royal couple still awaited a happy event.

Sandro continued to express his desire and hope.

But Celeste could feel that something within him had been extinguished, or at the very least, gone cold.

The giantess was caught between anger and guilt, powerless to bring to fruition what she so dearly desired.

To rid herself of these dark thoughts, Celeste would dedicate nearly all of her time to caring for the needy at the Chapel.

She would also write numerous letters to her family and the members of the troupe of the Vast World.

Dear Celeste. Everything is fine here at the farm, although I imagine it's nothing compared to the splendor of the court...

Her letters to her family only received rare replies, often arriving several months after hers.

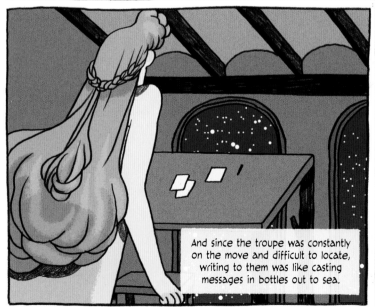

And since the troupe was constantly on the move and difficult to locate, writing to them was like casting messages in bottles out to sea.

For the first time in a long while, Celeste felt hopelessly alone.

Winter arrived at the same time the Queen Mother's ultimatum did.

HOW DARE SHE? THIS IS BARBARIC!

Do I parade the insides of her underwear before the entire city?

Don't talk about her that way, Celeste.

Why not? Do you approve of how she treats me?

She's not the only impatient one. The Master Boatmen and most of the city's inhabitants are eager to see me have a son.

To see YOU have a son?

You know what I mean...

How do you think not being able to get pregnant makes me feel?

To feel my barren womb, month after month, while my mind is full of what our child could become?

I'm sorry, but you're going to have to allow the andrologists to examine you.

WHAT?

I can't do anything to stop them anyway.

With their long beards and pointed hats, the andrologists always came in threes.

Uncontested experts in the secrets of fertility, they claimed they could prepare the female womb to bear male offspring.

Temperature, hygrometry, ventral inclination...

Carrot juice, catfish broth, nutritional frequency...

Astrology, tides, zodiac conjunctions...

Every detail counts!

But first, we must make sure that the uterus is suitable.

And that the terrain is fertile.

To overcome the humiliation of being exposed in such a fashion, Celeste forced herself to think of the future...

And the myriad of forms their future happiness would take.

Our verdict is final! No progeny shall ever spring forth from this body.

The Princess is sterile.

Sterile! Scarcely uttered, the word leaped from mouth to mouth before striking the giantess.

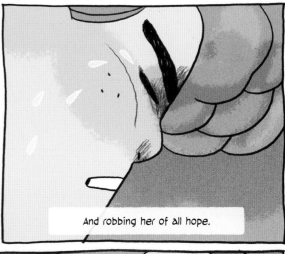

And robbing her of all hope.

In the days that followed, lawyers and jurists scoured civil codes and law books in a frenzy in order to decide what to do next.

Usually, a spouse's infertility is grounds for an annulment of the marriage.

But such a case has never been known to occur between two different species...

...the Princess remains legitimate.

Who said anything about annulling the marriage?! Let us not impose such a harsh dishonor upon the Princess.

She has but to agree to take the veil.

Of course! By entering a religious order, the Princess would enter into a union with the only being superior to the Prince: the Almighty.

And she would thus leave room for another wife.

It's out of the question, Sandro!

You can see that your mother is behind all of this.

We don't even know what those andrologist charlatans based their findings on...!

The Queen Mother has only the best interests of Dorsodoro in mind.

Sandro... no...

Know that the choice is yours, Princess. And I will respect it, whatever it is.

WHAT CHOICE ARE YOU TALKING ABOUT?!

How I wish things could be different...

NO!

Celeste was in despair. She didn't know what to do, or who to turn to.

Waves of violent rage swelled within her; she could almost picture herself crushing the Queen Mother...

Then she would regain control, overcome by painful, abysmal doubt: what if the andrologists were right?

Receiving a letter from the farm drove away her dark thoughts for a moment.

But only for a moment.

Oh no...

Ana and Jean were no more. Sixte informed her they had died shortly after one another, and hoped she would be present at their funeral.

The letter had been sent over two months ago.

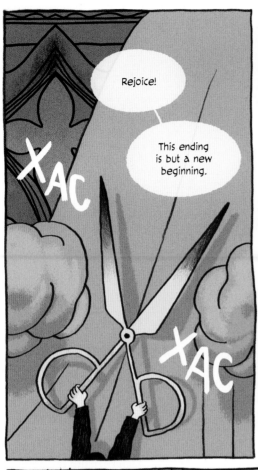

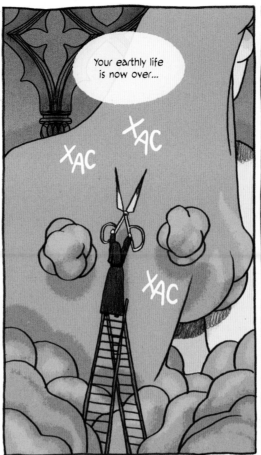

147

Chapter 10
The Convent of
Saint Eurexia

Of her journey to the High Lakes, Celeste recalled nothing but a vague memory, as if the cold and the first snows had covered everything.

The Mother Superior's welcome was as icy as the place itself.

In the cutting wind, she told them the tale of Eurexia, the Convent's patron saint.

How, set upon by pagans, she had refused to deny her faith.

How they had locked her away in a dark cave.

And how she had survived, deprived of everything, through the sheer strength of her prayers.

Each of you shall be given your own cell.

Carved into the very rock where Saint Eurexia accomplished her miracles.

Silence, darkness, contemplation.

The Saint's precepts shall reveal your true natures to you.

Forward, novice. Despite your outrageous size, you too shall one day come to know your place before the Almighty.

Without a word, Celeste entered her cell...

...as if in a hurry to vanish among its shadows.

Daily life in the Convent proved to be one of endless repetition, punctuated by prayers and chores.

At 4 a.m., the novices were awakened for Early Morning Prayer.

They would then tend to the animals until 7 a.m.

Then came Sunrise Prayer and the first light meal of the day.

Mornings were dedicated to the cleaning and maintenance of the Convent. No speaking was tolerated.

The midday meal was also taken in silence, preceded and followed by prayer.

Afternoons were devoted to study.

Our faith is the sustenance of the Almighty... The flesh is but an anchor.

In turn, novices and wise sisters would commit entire pages of Saint Eurexia's prayer book to memory.

At last, in the evenings, after briefly washing up, everyone would gather for a long vigil of prayers and hymns, which would sometimes continue late into the night.

It was in this manner that the Convent would possess its novices.

Its immutable order erased everything outside its walls.

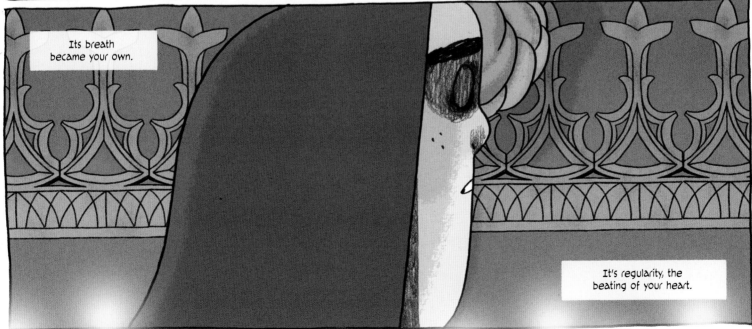

Its breath became your own.

It's regularity, the beating of your heart.

Pssst... Lady Celeste...

Here, take this. You need it much more than I do.

No, don't bother.

My name is Domenica. I come from Dorsodoro.

Your chapel often welcomed us. It is only fitting.

Those days are over! I require nothing!

But...?

SILENCE, NOVICES!

The night does not abide our splitting it with our frail voices.

Forty days after their arrival, the novices discovered that certain rituals followed somewhat longer patterns.

The Day of Breath has come. That of the Saved Truth!

One by one, you shall enter the tower of the Four Winds.

There you shall confess your sins, your failings, and your doubts to me, so that the Almighty may rid you of them forever.

Approach, novice, and reveal yourself.

153

Arise, novice.

Mother Superior?

It is time for you to learn the secret of this Sanctuary.

Only the wisest sisters and most fervent novices are allowed to enter this place.

It is a great privilege for you...

...to be allowed to meditate and pray in Her company.

A dark, fascinating flame was suddenly ignited within Celeste.

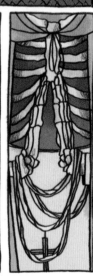

If you continue your efforts, you too shall be allowed to take the vow of silence and join us in contemplation.

A flame that licked at her insides.

And consumed her sadness.

It would be an honor.

154

With the arrival of the Winter Solstice, the Convent was plunged into a never-ending night...

...interspersed with a few short hours of half-light.

With tenfold rigor, Celeste constrained herself to fervent prayer and other privations...

...beneath the horrified, powerless gaze of Domenica.

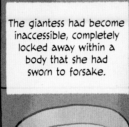

The giantess had become inaccessible, completely locked away within a body that she had sworn to forsake.

One morning, she did not attend Early Morning Prayer.

I'm coming in!

Domenica found her in the throes of a violent fever.

Beneath her tunic, a corset constricted her breasts.

NO!

We must take care of her! She needs our help.

It is not your place to do so, novice.

It is up to the Almighty to save...

...or to take away.

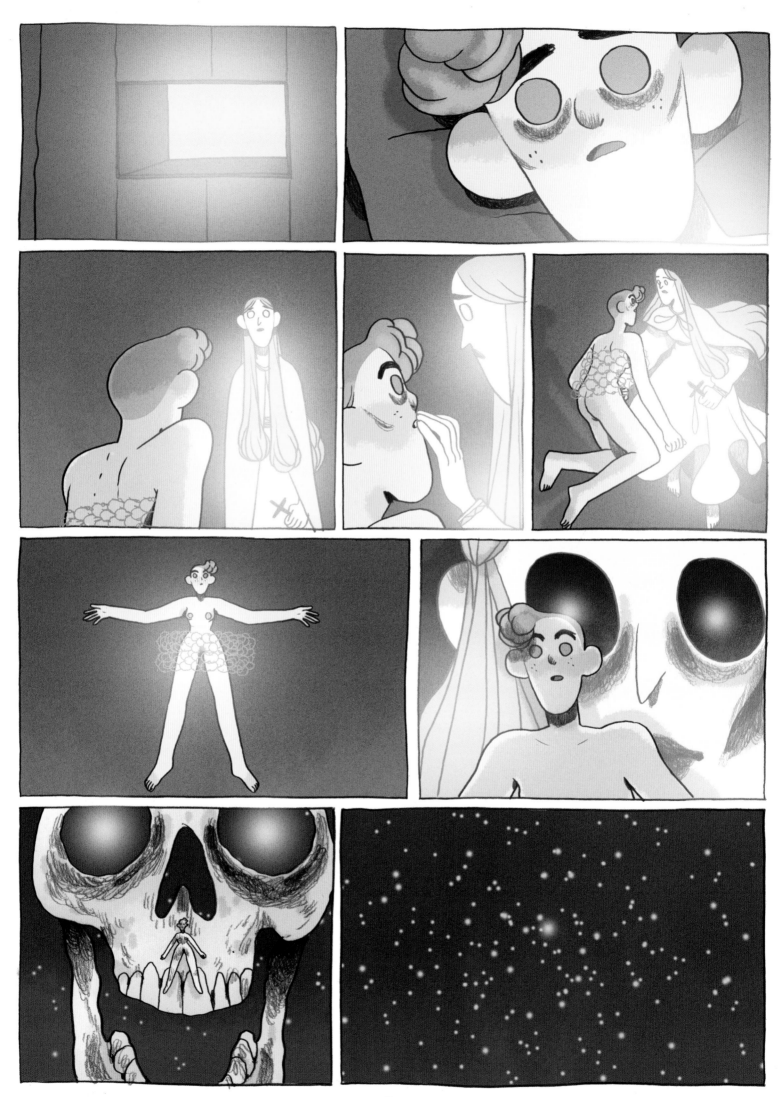

The first months of the year had brought their share of snow and ice, almost completely engulfing the Convent.

In this time of year, rare were the travelers who tried to reach it.

And rarer still were those who were accepted within.

Mother Superior, we are humble pilgrims who seek shelter for the night.

We share the Holy Word of the Only Book, and the icons of Saint Eurexia.

Men are forbidden in our convent, no matter how pious they are.

But night is approaching and a storm is threatening. Perhaps we might sleep in the stable with the animals?

You spoke of our Saint's icons?

We would be honored to offer them to you.

Bless you! We shall be warm here.

The visitors were right: a violent storm arose in the night.

Get up! It's time to go looking for her.

But that wasn't what kept them awake.

157

We need to search every cell. Hers shouldn't be hard to find.

That's for sure.

She's not inside.

What do you want with Lady Celeste?

Our intentions are pure! Be careful with that... uh... candle.

How do I know you're telling the truth?

I am Quintil, one of her brothers. I only wish to speak with her. She hasn't replied to any of my letters in months.

Mother Superior forbids any kind of communication with the outside.

I must see her. I have important news for her.

I think I know where she is.

But I'm not sure she will agree to see you.

What do you mean?

Domenica explained the events of the past few months to Quintil.

His face darkened as he heard each new revelation.

Even so, nothing could have prepared him for what he discovered inside the Sanctuary.

158

Celeste, it's me! Quintil! Your brother.

DESECRATION! MEN IN THE SANCTUARY!

We aren't looking for trouble! I just want to talk to my sister, Celeste.

Celeste has been purified, miscreant. And this novice has nothing more to say to you.

Isn't that so?

159

Celeste...

As for you, you are going to leave this sacred place immediately.

The night and the cold will take care of you.

No, you have no right!

The same goes for you!

BLAM!!

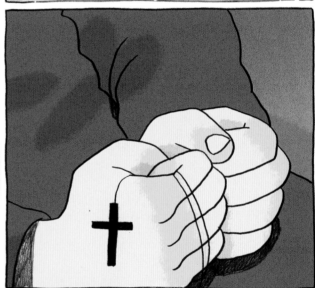

QUINTIL!!

QUINTIL!

Quintil! I'm so sorry!

It's me, Celeste! I should have come for you sooner.

Our... our parents, Quintil... I'm so ashamed!

Stop, little sister! No one blames you.

But I wasn't there to say goodbye to them.

They knew how much you loved them. They passed only a few weeks apart from each other, without suffering.

But I should have been there.

They loved each other too much to remain separated for long.

But you couldn't have been: for the simple reason that the Queen Mother intercepted all the letters we sent you.

She only let you have the cruelest ones, months too late.

Curse her!

His Serene Highness is the one who told me that. I was at Dorsodoro before coming here.

He entrusted all the letters he found to me and begs your forgiveness.

H... how is he?

I would say he puts on a brave face, but I believe he misses you.

He has sworn never to take another wife, much to his mother's dismay.

But...? What about the crown?

Power will be passed down to his nephew.

161

I... I don't even know why I'm crying anymore.

Everything is going to be fine, Celeste. As soon as the storm is over, we will recover our belongings and leave the High Lakes.

FUUOOOO

This novice is going nowhere! She has taken a vow of silence!

Her body belongs to Saint Eurexia!

Stop it!

NO!

Quintil!

Celeste!

Glory to the Almighty!

Saint Eurexia, give us strength!

STOP IT!

NO!

NO!

NO!

STOP IT!

NO!

BRAAAAM!!

BROOOOM!!

It's over, Celeste!

You are free once more!

Chapter 11
The Island of
the Mermaids

After leaving Saint Eurexia, Celeste realized she was going to need time.

She found it by the seashore, in Bonaccorso, the quiet village where Quintil had opened his print shop and bookstore.

Time for the warmth of the sun and the vastness of the sea...

Time to find peace and to understand...

Time to find herself again.

Every day, Quintil would bring her both physical and spiritual nourishment.

Together, they would talk of their childhood memories, and eagerly awaited Tertio's annual stopover in the village's small harbor.

165

The weeks stretched out, identical and peaceful, in the balmy climate.

She felt like she could gladly spend her whole life this way.

When is Tertio coming to meet us?

I don't really know, Celeste.

You should tell her the truth, Quintil...

What truth are you talking about, Eurylocus? They're only rumors!

Is there a problem?

Rumors are the foam on the surface of truth.

There are rumors that Tertio's ship has disappeared.

WHAT?

It's no mere disappearance! The Mermaids have taken them!

Your brother had planned on navigating much too close to their island.

That's why I refused to embark with him.

Complete nonsense!

Fish-women... What will they think of next?

A 60-foot-tall giantess?

166

167

For the first time in a long while, Celeste seethed with anger and worry.

But at the same time, a tenacious thought floated on the surface of her doubts.

Tertio needed her.

It was high time she left to go help him.

Celeste set off without thinking, swimming straight towards the setting sun.

The months spent swimming in the sea had strengthened her body, and the giantess felt capable of going on for days at a time.

The provisions and water on the raft would allow her to hold out for at least several weeks.

The first night was splendid.

The days that followed were uneventful, and Celeste even met unexpected companions.

The problems began on the seventh night.

In the heart of the storm, Celeste discovered how small she truly was.

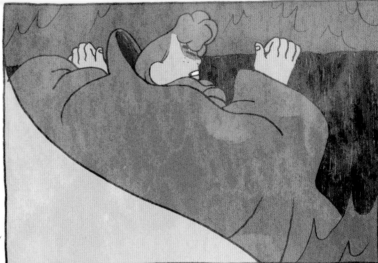

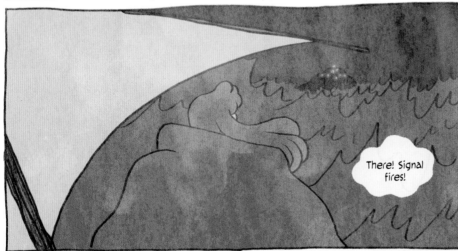

There! Signal fires!

Redoubling her efforts, she managed to head towards them...

...before realizing that there were worse dangers than the waves.

CRAJH!!

My...
my leg...

Help!

The melodious songs of birds, the softness of a freshly-made bed, enchanting smells...

When Celeste opened her eyes, she first thought she had reached the afterlife.

We bid you welcome, O Celeste!

We welcome you among your own kind.

You... you're giantesses?

We are only women. But we strive to walk as tall as possible.

How do you know my name?

Your experiences and exploits have been whispered to us on the trade winds, and by our messenger birds.

I am Hapis, the Phoenix of this Island.

Mine is the duty to lead our community for a cycle of forty moons.

Ten bird-mistresses, each of whom specializes in a special domain, stand ready to help me.

Falca takes care of the hunting, Luscine, of the arts, and Caladre, of healing.

It is she who treated your leg wound.

Before the new moon rises, you shall walk again.

That will give you time to discover our island and to decide if your place is here.

My place?

You haven't come to join the community?

In truth, I am looking for Tertio, my brother.

He is a sailor. I hoped he had landed here.

On the Island of Mermaids, there are no men.

Since they are behind every act of oppression we have suffered, we have chosen to live exclusively among women. And by doing so, we have achieved complete freedom.

171

But perhaps you saw his ship?

We take steps to ensure they stay far from our shores.

Furthermore, we have become experts in the art of creating fog over the waves.

An old woman taught me how. A certain Laelith.

You know her? Is she here?

No, but I was her disciple, a long time ago.

And her teachings have served as a model for our island.

As soon as you have recovered, I will show you how we live here.

Until then, you still require rest.

Tertio, Laelith, the bird-women... Celeste fell asleep with their faces swirling about her.

Caladre's treatments soon bore their fruits, and Celeste was able to explore the island.

This island is by no means large, but it is more than enough to provide for the needs of the thousand women who live here.

We separate into four groups whose duties change with every moon.

The first group takes care of our food, with Garuda overseeing agriculture and harvesting...

...and Bassane, the fishing.

The second group is tasked with preparing these resources for use by the rest of us: daily meals, reserves, clothing, and tools.

172

The third group devotes itself to education and learning.

Books being rare, we decided to engrave all of our knowledge upon giant murals, located all around the island.

Thus, at any time during our walks, we may acquire new knowledge.

What...? There are children here, too?

Of course! Many women who come here are pregnant or have young children. We find a place for them in the Nest, a building that is reserved for them.

You accept little boys here, too?

Up until their tenth year. They must then leave the island. More often than not, their mothers leave with them.

What about the fourth group?

Swimming, games, relaxation. Freedom for everyone goes hand in hand with the individual having the freedom to do whatever she wishes.

That's very true...

As for those women there, they interpret the birds' flight patterns to catch glimpses of the future.

The birds can sense much more than we can. They foretold your coming, in fact.

Really?

Of course...

This... this is incredible...

173

Celeste continued to make a steady recovery, and each day revealed another new and surprising aspect of how life was organized on the island.

Each inhabitant seemed to blossom at her own pace, while all of them progressed together in the fields of mutual aid and coeducation.

Even the giantess herself was given a taste of the joys of teaching.

And yet, Tertio never left her thoughts. But none of the women she questioned had seen a ship on the horizon.

Was Quintil right after all? Perhaps Tertio had already even arrived back in Bonaccorso!

AAAAH!!

?!

Nando?

¡¡AAAARK!!

SCHOOP!

NO!

TSSHHT!

You caught him?

Yes. Without trouble.

Where did he come from? I thought there were no men on the island?

Shall I take him back to the Lower Courtyard?

Lower Courtyard? What are you talking about?

I would have preferred talking about this under other circumstances...

But perhaps this is a sign, after all.

The Lower Courtyard is where we keep the males that are necessary for the community's reproductive needs.

You keep them locked up?

We take very good care of them.

They are fed, cared for, and have access to many varied forms of entertainment.

We have them parade about regularly, and we organize harmless sparring matches for them.

They love them! It stimulates them.

And when one of us desires them, she chooses one that suits her, and he joins her to copulate.

Why does she wear a mask?

Pleasure is necessary. Feelings are forbidden.

Certain males are here of their own free will.

And many others would fight to lead such a life.

That wasn't the case of your fugitive.

Perhaps the time has come for him to leave the island.

What about my brother? Is he here?

In order to be truly free, you must break all ties to males. Including those of blood.

You're completely mad...

TERTIO!!

TSSHHFT!

What...?!

You need to think. Spending some time in the palace will help you.

This time, when Celeste awoke, she was certain she had not reached the afterlife.

HAPIS!

You have no right to do this!

HAPIS!

Save your breath.

You're going to need it to escape.

Falca?

I am going to allow you to free the males and make your way to the western tip of the island.

There you will find the hidden boat that Hapis uses when she needs to return to the mainland.

Why are you helping me?

The males must leave this island for good. Hapis has transgressed her own law.

For the bird-women to be truly free, we must follow our ideals through to the very end.

But you will be condemned to extinction!

I don't believe so. The shipwrecks we cause on stormy nights will more than satisfy our needs for males.

You're as mad as she is.

Hurry up before I change my mind.

TERTIO?

A new suitress!

Without a mask!

It will take a real man to satisfy her.

Celeste!

TERTIO!

We're leaving the island! All of us together!

And what makes you think I want to leave?

The fact that they'll kill any of you who remain behind?

What of our children?

I was traveling with my daughter and my son when we were shipwrecked here.

I'm not leaving without them.

Me neither!

Nor will I!

Fine! We'll go get them at the Nest.

A hot, howling wind had arisen on the island...

...but even those heavy gusts could not cover the joyful cries of their reunion.

PAPA!

My daughter!

We must hurry!

I... I'm sorry...

Nando?

I wanted to apologize for all the trouble I caused you... I'm not worthy of your help.

We... we'll talk about that later. We must leave.

Where are you going?

Back to dry land.

Can we come with you even if we don't have parents?

Of course! Anyone who wants to leave the island may join us.

You aren't going anywhere unless the Phoenix allows it!

How dare you claim to carry on Laelith's legacy? Your island is nothing but a sinister prison that enslaves men and conditions women.

It is the exact opposite of the males' world! And as such, it restores the balance!

It reproduces it without surpassing it!

Enough! Send them all to heaven!

KRRAASSHH!!

NO! NO!

Fanned by the wind, the flames swiftly transformed the palace into an immense inferno.

Celeste led the way, desperately searching for a cove or harbor...

...with the ever-growing fear that Falca might have lied to her.

But it's not big enough for us all.

Down there! I see a boat...

Pile into it! I'll swim behind you.

With your hurt leg?

I THOUGHT I TOLD YOU TO LEAVE THE ISLAND!

180

Chapter 12
The Tatterdemalions

Their return to Bonaccorso was both joyful and emotional.

Families were finally reunited, after long years of separation.

Others were spontaneously formed with generous immediacy.

All of the inhabitants, in one way or another, warmly welcomed the castaways, offering food, clothing, and shelter.

Quintil opened the doors of his bookstore to the children, and Celeste's cave was transformed into a vast makeshift camp filled with laughter, games, and roughhousing.

The arrival of the cold season altered people's behavior.

Joy turned to indifference...

Indifference to impatience...

And impatience to resentment.

They've been leeching off of us for over three months, now!

The harvests weren't meant to feed so many!

Celeste understood that once again, the time had come to move on.

But now she was no longer alone. And the Island of Mermaids had awakened strange possibilities within her.

Why not wait until springtime? They will have changed their minds by then.

You know very well that won't happen.

We could go back to sea?

There are too many of us. And the journey would be too perilous.

But I have another idea.

What kind of idea?

You'll see soon enough...

And so it was that Celeste once again took to the road, followed by those who would soon be called the Tatterdemalions.

Wherever they passed, the group was welcomed with curiosity and benevolence.

Everyone wanted to see the giantess and her thousand orphans.

Naturally, the Tatterdemalions quickly attracted newcomers.

Isolated mothers, lost men... Celeste accepted them all in her wake.

After several weeks of walking, they finally discovered their destination.

Dorsodoro.

Are you sure you're ready to come back here?

Absolutely!

The City of Water is in mourning. The Queen Mother is dead.

Sandro's nephew shall soon be crowned.

Sandro! He will help us.

CELESTE!

I dreamt of this moment so many times!

I will never forgive myself for what I did to you...

We could accuse each other of so many things...

...and of so many things that were out of our control.

Oh, Celeste! You alone are worthy of the title of Serene Highness.

Titles no longer interest me.

I just want to reopen my Chapel and welcome all those who are in need.

That's a wonderful idea. But the Chapel will be far too small.

You'll need a place worthy of you.

The Chapel may be cramped, but we will make do.

Here!

This is an untouched valley in the princely domain. It's all yours.

Amaurota.

It's too much, Sandro!

It's nothing compared to what I inflicted upon you.

And I know you will turn it into something wonderful.

I belong to Dorsodoro. And the future Serene Highness is going to need my help.

Come with us!

Thank you, my Prince...

Celeste and her Tatterdemalions now had a goal: a land in which they could realize all their hopes and dreams.

One evening, as they set up camp on the outskirts of a village, the past caught up with them once again.

Celeste!?

Nina! Tirso! Are you performing nearby?

Let's just say that after a few shows, we heard tell that the Mother of Thousands was nearby.

It could only be you!

The Mother of Thousands! Is that what they're calling me?

Men often come up with catchy nicknames...

And Alto? Is he still with you?

Still among the clouds, little one!

Day after day, the road to the valley of Amaurota brought Celeste ever closer to familiar landscapes.

Memories came rushing back, reflected suddenly in the rays of the sun.

One morning, Celeste decided to take a double detour.

The first was to her childhood farm, where Sixte now lived with his own family...

...and where she knelt for a long time in quiet reflection before her parents' shared grave.

The second detour took her near the Archdiocese, to the White Knight of Parangon's unchanged castle.

Lady Celeste! You have returned at last!

It's not what you think, Parangon. I'm only passing through.

My hair has turned white, my library takes up even more room, but my feelings for you remain unchanged!

Really? You swear that there has been no other woman in your life, in all these years?

Well... beugh... almost...

No one like you, in any case!

How reassuring! Promises must never become prisons.

So why have you returned?

I want you to come with us! To build, organize, and awaken the imaginations of all these children.

Books, furniture, horses, we will bring whatever you want with us...

I don't know what to say...

But living by your side is all that I have ever aspired to.

You'll have to share me, Parangon.

Any fragment of your attention will be enough to fill me with joy.

I knew I could count on you, Sir Knight.

The giantess and her Tatterdemalions resumed their march, allowing the newcomers to familiarize themselves with living conditions within the group.

The buttresses of Amaurota appeared during the final weeks of winter.

At first, the ascension seemed easy.

The nearness of their destination strengthened everyone tenfold.

And it was only thanks to Celeste's determination...

But the first complications soon hindered their progression.

The reason the valley was isolated soon became apparent.

...her intelligence...

...and her generosity that they reached the final pass that led to Amaurota.

We're almost there!

The Titan's Pass!

Your Prince certainly gave you a rather odd gift...

We'll never be able to overcome such a monster.

I'll pave the way.

Despite the icy wind, Celeste calmly approached the cliff.

A daughter of the mountaintops, she felt herself on familiar ground.

She had nearly reached her goal. Soon, the valley would become a new home for all those who had followed her.

She was born of the mountain. And the mountain would never betray her.

KRRAAKK

At least that's what she thought, until she began to fall.

AAAAHH!!

All together, now!

And, in a way, she was right.

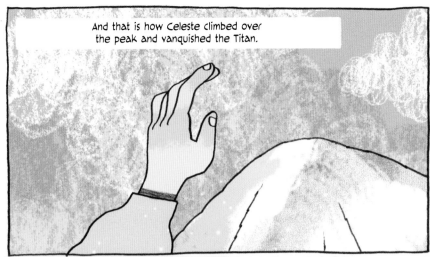
And that is how Celeste climbed over the peak and vanquished the Titan.

Amaurota spread out before her, immense and unspoiled.

There was so much to be done and imagined!

The first days were chaotic and joyful.

Celeste promptly assigned tasks to one and all...

Everyone contributed according to his skills.

Or passions.

Little by little, the beginnings of a city began to take shape, even taking on a new name.

Our city shall be called Laelith from this day forth!

One summer afternoon, a new arrival appeared.

SANDRO!

I've done a great deal of thinking, Celeste. I want to live with you. With all of you.

There will be no prince here. Nor castle.

That's precisely what I seek.

To forget the Serene Highness and find out who Sandro truly is.

I, too, can't wait to find out...

Over the following months, the number of Laelith's inhabitants grew.

Celeste refused to enclose the city within restrictive walls.

Our city must remain open to others and to the sounds of the world.

Children, adults, girls or boys, all were given a fair and equal education.

Upon reaching adulthood, they could choose to make their home in the city, in the valley...

...or to leave and discover the vast world outside.

Celeste lived simply, among the other inhabitants, sharing her time among her three men.

She would come and go according to their shared, respected desires.

Surrounded by both men and women alike, the giantess felt she had found her place at last.

One morning, at daybreak, Celeste began to climb up to the valley's highest mountaintop.

Far below, Laelith and its inhabitants were slowly waking up.

Nature was breathtakingly beautiful.

Having reached the summit, she stood still.

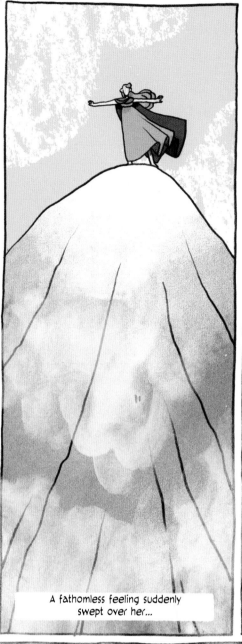

A fathomless feeling suddenly
swept over her...

A feeling of harmony
and freedom...

...that uplifted her
to the heavens.

I
The Twin Stars
Nando's Comet
II
The Six Brothers
The Dragon of Alicastre
III
The Three Princes